THE
STORY
OF
YOU

How Your Story Can Power Your Success

Pelè Raymond Ugboajah, PhD

For Reki, Ijeoma, Obi, and Ikenna

Contents

At every crossroad, follow your dream.
It is courageous to let your heart lead the way.
– LELAND THOMAS

Prologue

Story is magical. It is the one form of communication our human species understands from the moment we first begin to use languages. Whether you're three or ninety-three, something trancelike happens in your mind and spirit when you hear the words, "once upon a time." Everyone agrees: story helps us make sense of the world. No matter who we are, or where we come from, story helps us find meaning in our lives.

But wait!

What if this concept of story - which we viscerally envision as something that we hear over a campfire, or see in a movie, or read in a newspaper - what if story is much more than that? What if hidden inside every person's story is a powerful, transformative code – a discernable database of lessons and structural phases – that we can assess and use to proactively create lasting leadership and success in our lives?

This is what my research tells me. Your story is not just some random series of life events that will inevitably roll off into the forgotten annals of history. Your story is a repository of unique lessons and a creative template for deciding your life's purpose, designing lasting leadership and success, and fulfilling your destiny. Story might just be the most important gift that humankind has ever received.

I invite you to journey with me into your deepest reservoir of personal and professional success ... the story of you.

Pelè Raymond Ugboajah, PhD

THE

STORY

OF

YOU

How Your Story Can Power Your Success

1.

Life Is A Story

Life is not about finding yourself. Life is about creating yourself.
– GEORGE BERNARD SHAW.

Once upon a time, my father died. I couldn't believe it, but there he was, and it was true. Only a few days ago, I had seen him, sat with him, and eaten dinner with him. I *laughed* with him. But today, his body was here, blank, cold. He was gone. I had no tears, only wide-eyed shock. As I passed his coffin for the last time, something in my young mind snapped into place. In a very personal way, something you and I already know very well became vividly clear to me. This life – this existence we share – is extremely terminal. My life was changed forever. I now knew that someday, we all go where my father went that day.

Life actually ends.

I remember how different people walked up to me that day, and told me various pieces of my father's story. Each one of them described him; when they first met him, what he was like, and what his legacy was. With tears in their eyes, they all felt a strong, palpable need to tell me the story of my father.

That was when I first realized that life is a story.

Think of yourself on the morning of your last day on earth. Picture yourself as a ninety-five year-old, lying on your deathbed, still able to think back many, many years to younger days. Do you see a happy, fulfilled, deeply satisfied you? Or do you see pain and regret across your brow as you recall the many things you should have, or could have done with your life? What story will your mind be frantically rummaging through?

> **What will be the story of you?**

Someday, everyone's story will be told, and each one of us will be responsible for how our stories turn out. We can either proactively design our story today, or stand back and watch it unfold by default. This is a book about how to *create* the story of you today, and how to use that story to power whatever future success you desire. If you want to have a hand in how your story turns out, you may want to consider Stephen Covey's advice, and start living with the end in mind (Covey, 1989).

As an artist carefully sketches fine lines, gradually increasing their strength until an image is birthed, this book will show you how to bring forth whatever story you desire for yourself. And like an artist, you will need a structure, a template, or a series of predictable sequences and principles that you can use to slowly mold that story into shape. What this book offers is a simple contribution: the structure for creating your story is the story itself.

Let me explain.

Everyone has a story. Every story has a beginning, middle, and an end. For good or for bad, your life has exactly the same components and potential as any of the greatest stories ever told. Think of the stories of Braveheart, The Titanic, Star Wars, Things Fall Apart, Martin Luther King, Gandhi, Mandela, Jesus, and a host of other powerful epics. Your life has the same narrative elements as these timeless stories, except for three important details. First, your story is neither a history, nor a fiction, nor an adventure told by someone else. It is a tangible, ongoing, dynamic narrative that is unfolding before your very eyes – every single day. Second, you have more control over your evolving story than you can imagine. And third, you are faced with a daily, critical choice: either *watch* your story happen, or *make* it happen.

If you're like most people, at some point in your life, you have nurtured dreams and visions of doing the things you love, finding fulfillment, and contributing to society in your own special way. Yet like so many, you have probably left most of those dreams behind, and you are now much more pragmatic – making do in a world of seemingly limited choices. Far too many people merely exist in lives they do not love, doing work they love even less, and getting by each month, one paycheck away from poverty and disaster.

I'm here to tell you that there is much more to life than that.

There is potential for great success and deep fulfillment inside of you that lies mostly untapped and forgotten, waiting for the day that someone, somewhere, will open the door and let it come through. That special day you've been waiting for is today, the place is here, and that someone is *you*.

For Whom This Book Was Written

Are you one of those folks who have always known *exactly* what they wanted to be from an early age? Are you one of those who got into their chosen career right out of school and became happy, fulfilled, successful leaders in the exact field and vocation they always had a passion for? If you're one of those folks, then this book may not be for you, and from most statistics I've seen, you are definitely in the minority. Most people struggle for some time with the question of what exactly their purpose is on this planet.

If you're an employee, I have a question for you. Are you *passionate* about your job? If your answer is yes, you are once again in the minority. In a nationwide survey of 7,718 American workers, only 20% of them reported that they were 'passionate' about their work (PR Newswire, 2008). Wouldn't it be wonderful to live life and go to work each day with a clear passion for what you do?

I was one of those people who struggled at finding their purpose – and that's putting it mildly! I'm pretty sure if you count all my employment stints and entrepreneurial ventures, I easily exceeded the national average of ten job 'changes' in a lifetime. If, like me, you've ever had to do some experimentation to figure yourself out, and if you would like to learn a proven way to more quickly liberate the potential within you, read on.

Ultimately, we're talking about leadership – but not the standard form that involves the followership of others – rather, our focus is on self-leadership. There is strong evidence in life and the workplace that the first step to any great achievement starts with leadership. But you cannot effectively lead others, *until you are able to lead yourself!* You can't sell a vision to others if you aren't already solidly convinced of it yourself. As Maxwell Maltz said, "the most important sale in life is to sell yourself to yourself."

> **This book is about the first step in leadership: Self-leadership.**

In most organizations today, leadership is in great demand but short supply. A survey of Chief Human Resource Officers indicated that 80% of them don't believe their organizations develop leaders well (HR Policy Association, 2008). Another survey found that 50% of top executives are dissatisfied with their work (ExecuNet, 2007).

Why is it so difficult to find, retain, and develop great leaders?

The reason is that our selection and development methods do not go deep enough into people's stories. It's not easy to identify great leadership potential from a resume, a few psychological tests, or a set of predefined leadership competencies. You also can't pick great leaders solely on charisma, or even their ability to influence others. You have to include in the discovery mix, a sincere effort at listening to their stories.

Great leaders are best recognized through the self-leadership stories they've lived, and the current self-story they espouse. Great leaders are successful self-leaders because they have first found unshakable clarity in their own purpose, passion, lessons-learned, and vision for the future. Great leaders *know* their stories. If you want to find, retain, and develop great leaders, you have to really *listen* to them.

This book follows the premise that your leadership potential and life success are hidden as codes in the story you've already lived – waiting to be unleashed. The tools and instructions for achieving your greatest destiny have been with you all along – written in your heart, and unfolding daily in the story of *you*.

Here is a list of groups who can benefit from this book:

1. People in search of their life's unique purpose, either as individuals, in the workplace, or as aspiring entrepreneurs.

2. Leaders who want to identify high potential employees and put the right people in the right jobs.

3. Organizations seeking to prepare emerging leaders for future leadership roles.

4. Educational Institutions seeking to prepare their students for successful future careers.

Why This Book Was Written

This book is a right-brained, story-driven contribution to a leadership development field that has become dominated by left-brained, psychological assessment processes dedicated more to finding *'what's wrong'* with people, rather than *'what's great'* about them. My approach, while deceptively simple, fills an important gap in how we select, retain, and develop leaders today. The 'story of you' process helps people explore and expand their potential from the viewpoint that a person's story contains reservoirs of greatness – an approach that is sorely lacking among today's outmoded, cookie-cutter leadership development processes.

There are therefore two main uses for this book:

1. Through a more qualitative, narrative approach, people can learn how to use their personal stories to power their self-leadership, personal fulfillment, and future success, however they may define it for themselves.

2. Simultaneously, organizations can use this narrative process to cull richer leadership competency data from their subjects during selection, retention, and development efforts.

Consider the following Cable Network News story. It featured a tragic picture of a former executive who now stands on New York street corners, dressed in a suit, and looking for a job with a sign that says, "Almost Homeless" (CNN, 2008).

Now, imagine this man – who could be anyone in today's economy – finally getting an opportunity to interview for a job. What would he be asked at the interview? What would he say? How accurate do you think the information-gathering will be?

Most likely, his resume will be his main source of information in a business landscape where 57% of surveyed hiring managers said they have caught lies on a resume (CareerBuilder, 2006).

He will probably also experience unstructured interviews designed to determine his personality or leadership 'fit' in the organization. And if the organization provides him the standard psychological assessment tests, he will probably feel like he's being hooked up to a lie-detector machine.

This is no way to find and retain top leaders!

Yet, the one thing that is missing from the assessment mix – his story – could be the best way to get valuable information about his 'fit' in the organization. For example, look at the one story we already know about this man. We know that he is enterprising, innovative, and not afraid to challenge the status quo. How do we know this? Because by standing on the corner, he was living a leadership story in real-time.

What we don't know about him may be the most valuable 'fit' information of all, such as his life's purpose, what he's passionate about, his life's lessons, and what his personal vision for the future is. All of which are only accessible through a qualitative, in-depth process of 'listening' to his story.

Resumes and psychological assessments alone provide only a snapshot, a small part of the story. Organizations need to get the whole story if they want to make good, sustainable decisions for attracting, retaining, and developing talent. Stories – not resumes or psychological tests alone – are the single most useful repository of leadership information.

What I Learned From My Story

My viewpoints have evolved predominantly from four sources of experience: (a) common themes observed while working with my executive coaching clients, (b) my research in leadership, narrative, neuroscience, and positive psychology, (c) by examining some of the greatest stories of all time, and (d) through the experience of my own circuitous story.

I have found many parallels in the story patterns from disparate worlds of fiction, religion, politics, and business that mirrored what was going on in my own life, and in the lives of my coaching clients. In the next few chapters I'll introduce these patterns, and demonstrate how they offer a powerful framework for designing and fueling your future success.

But first, here's a synopsis of *my* story.

I started life as a refugee child in a war-torn African village, and through countless trials and tribulations, I worked my way up to the highest reaches of the American dream. My given name was Pelè – after the world-famous Brazilian soccer player – even though as a child, I couldn't play soccer to save my life! Instead, I had a passion for storytelling and a desire to use my talents of art, music, and literature to help others live out their purpose.

Yet for years I ignored the direct use of my own God-given talents, seeking instead the perceived status and comfort of corporate management titles and six-figure salaries. The result of not clearly figuring out my own purpose over the years was that no matter how far I got professionally or financially, whether collecting a fat paycheck, driving around in a brand new Range Rover, or lounging in a sprawling pond-side home, I was never quite fulfilled inside.

My life had become dangerously similar to what was described in an article I read the other day about Alec Baldwin, who at 50, was "disappointed" with himself despite the fact that he was one of the richest, and most famous actors in Hollywood (The New Yorker, 2008). Perhaps he and I suffered from the lack of fulfillment that comes from living by default, rather than by design.

My challenge could be summed up by the following question:

> "What will it profit a man if he gains the whole world, and loses his own soul?" – Mark 8:36 NKJV

But I got lucky.

After years of education, journeying all the way to a doctorate degree, and after decades of toil in corporate middle management and an assortment of entrepreneurial careers, I finally experienced a personal and professional breakthrough.

I found *my* story!

And it was more powerful than anything I had ever imagined.

I found that my story wasn't really about my degrees or corporate titles. It also had nothing to do with financial rewards. My story involved core passions I held deep inside for art, music, teaching, and writing books – all storytelling skills – and all of which I had previously swept under the rug in pursuit of material success.

If you've ever watched the movie 'Gladiator', you'll remember when Commodus entered the arena of the amphitheatre, and asked the battle-worn slave warrior to take off his mask and reveal himself. After initially refusing, the gladiator finally did so in front of thousands, at the risk of losing his life. But when he did so – when he finally answered his true name – his story was liberated. What once was lost was found, and he confronted the purpose of his very existence. He was no longer just 'the Spaniard', or 'gladiator'. He was Maximus Decimus Meridius, the most celebrated general of his time, protector of Rome, and ready to sacrifice his life to return honor and fair rule to the burning empire.

Like Maximus, I found my name.

I was Pelè, a *storyteller*.

I discovered not only my past story, but also my metaphor for the future. Soccer became more than a game for me. It became my symbol for teaching people what I think is the most important leadership development skill of all, which I now call:

LeaderPractice.

This breakthrough was so strong that it empowered me to take the audacious step of abandoning the artificial security of a six-figure salary and starting from scratch as a humble writer, musician, and teacher. I have since found my place in the world, and it was a simple, potent idea that liberated me from the constraints and faulty assumptions of materialism.

The idea I discovered is this:

> Success is not an achievement.
> It is the story we tell ourselves.

Purpose, Passion, Lessons, And Success

This book will describe the structure and the principles you'll need for identifying and clarifying your life's purpose, passion, and lessons, all of which are foundational elements for designing and implementing your future success story. These critical success elements are never easy to decipher from standard psychological assessments, but can all be readily found by examining one's already-lived life story. Since we'll be using these words quite a bit, some concise definitions are in order.

First, what is your life's purpose?

This has to be the single biggest question that people face in their lives. Some have no sense of purpose, and are constantly swayed by the winds of circumstance. Others may have declared a purpose, but it is the 'wrong' one for their lives in the sense that it is driven from the external, and not congruent with whom they truly are inside. In both cases, the challenge many people face is that they have not done enough introspective research to figure out exactly what their life's purpose ought to be.

I believe that *purpose* is the reason you showed up on this planet, and it is unique to every single one of us. It is our responsibility to understand it, nurture it, and manifest it. If we don't, we'll always wonder why we wake up each morning. Life can't always be about survival, or about making a few dollars just to pay the bills. There is much more to life, and it is revealed when you know and implement your life's unique purpose.

> "It is our responsibility to manifest what is planted in our hearts"
>
> – Kojo Benjamin Taylor

What are you truly passionate about?

Passion is that magical, emotional component that powers human success. Descartes had it wrong when he wrote, "I think, therefore I am." In fact, there is overwhelming scientific evidence that emotions play a much greater role in our decisions, actions, and lives than was previously assumed in conventional, western wisdom. We are not thinking beings who feel; we are feeling beings who think. If you can find your passion – your "bliss" as Joseph Campbell would say – if you can locate that set of emotions that will make every single day something to look forward to, you will be much more productive and success-bound (Campbell, 1990). It is folly to ignore the power of your own internal emotions.

What lessons have you learned?

Life presents us with lessons that are uniquely ours. If we learn these lessons, we move on to new ones. If we don't learn our lessons, we end up finding ourselves back at square one, facing the same lessons all over again. The key to forward movement is to learn our lessons, and build upon them for future success. Your past story has a rich database of lessons that form the core of what you should, or should not be doing in your current and future story. You have to study those lessons and decide what to use or discard, but in general, there are no mistakes in life – just lessons.

What does success mean to you?

We are conditioned by society to define and measure success through the accolades we receive, the degrees we earn, the titles we claim, and the wealth we stash away. Yet none of these *outward* achievements will bring true, enduring fulfillment. Only an internal, non-materialistic definition of success will allow you to find fulfillment and peace of mind. Externally adopted, acquisitive definitions usually lead to agony and peer pressure.

Success is therefore not about *arriving* somewhere; quite to the contrary, there is no endpoint. There is no destination – no *there,* there. Rather, success is about being on the right journey and doing what you love. It is easy to do a lot of things right, and yet not be doing the *right* thing for *your* life.

> Success is about being in the right story.

The Story Of You

All of my life, I have been an artist, whether through fine art, music, literature, or as a speaker. From all of these creative pursuits I have found one common truth:

Creativity requires three levels of activity.

The first level involves a creation of the end product in the mind. The second level involves the structured, documented design of that end product. And the third level involves the actualization of that design through action. Through all of these levels, you need a framework and a set of guiding principles upon which the design can occur. These same rules apply for creating your future success story.

The 'story of you' is the *right* success story for *your* life, and it is the one that will bring you enduring fulfillment. In the following pages, you'll find that I'm offering a discussion about three broad skills and twelve underlying principles for making your story:

1. **Story-Listening**: Your already-lived life contains clues about three foundational success principles: your *purpose, personality*, and *lessons*. Your past story is an assessment resource, and to access its rich reservoir of information, you must engage in Story-Listening.

2. **Story-Writing**: From what you learn about yourself, you can design a successful future by relying on a framework made from the same phases that can be found in any story. These phases are your story's *context, challenge, change, conclusion*, and *contribution*. Using this universal structure as a guide for designing your future success is called Story-Writing.

3. **Story-Practicing**: Once you design your future story, you have to engage in actions that help you 'sell' it to yourself and 'practice' it until your unconscious powers are motivated to guide you to your goals. Story-Practicing involves a continuing focus on four activities; acting out your *self-story*, pursuing *goals*, maximizing *strengths*, and minimizing *weaknesses*.

These three skills and twelve principles are represented in the following 'story wheel', and will serve as the organizing system for the sections and chapters of this book.

Now, let's look at how the various principles and dimensions in your story can work together to power your success.

(1). Story-Listening

Your story contains important qualitative information about your strengths and weaknesses, which are the first building blocks for designing your future. To gain access to this information, you have to go beyond the standard psychological assessment tests, and leverage the *inner* truths hidden in your story. These stories from your past and present will do much to help reveal your purpose, passions, and lessons-learned.

This process, which I call *Story-Listening*, is a combination of the following assessment processes:

- Purpose (the confluence of your skills, passion, and success experiences).

- Personality (what you, others, and your life decisions say about you).

- Lessons (what your life has uniquely taught you).

I once experienced a rigorous personality assessment process prior to getting hired into a corporate job. I had a great, skills-based résumé, and I remember how accurate the multi-rater psychological results proved to be about certain outward, behavioral aspects of my life. However, no one asked me much about my life's purpose, my burning passions, or the lessons I had learned about myself throughout my already-lived life. Yet these were the very reasons why I eventually left that particular job – to pursue what I felt was in fact my true calling.

Both the hiring company and I would have saved a lot of time and effort, not to mention money, if we had engaged in a more thorough, qualitative *story* assessment.

(2). Story-Writing

All of life is a story; and you are an evolving story that will someday be told by others. When your story is told, it will have the same patterns as any story that has ever been told. Why not use those universal patterns for how stories are made and told, to design and live your own story today?

If you think about it, you'll find that your life's narrative has essentially the same structure as Hansel and Gretel, David and Goliath, The Lord of the Rings, The Wizard of Oz, or any other story. What makes those stories great is not only *what* happened in them; what makes them great is the *structure* of how things happened in them.

Once upon a time, life was good. Something happened. Trouble appeared. You, the hero, arrived. Change began. The world was saved. *You* were saved.

There is something universal about how stories are structured, which is why we relate to them so easily, and why they can help us to more efficiently design our *self-story* and *goals* as they unfold before us.

This universal story pattern, which I call the 'Five Acts', is as follows:

- Context
- Challenge
- Change
- Conclusion
- Contribution.

These five 'acts' are the same patterns you will find in any literary story, adapted to the requirements of self-leadership and your own self-story. The only difference is that, in this story, you are the hero, and you will play the self-leadership roles required to make your story a success.

This pattern provides a structure for planning your success. In the field of medicine for example, practically every diagnosis involves pattern identification. When you can predict patterns, you don't always have to know all of the details in order to recommend proactive actions. You may not know what will happen in the future, but you can ensure better outcomes if you model and follow proven story patterns. This method of planning your success story – while you're still living it – therefore involves taking what you learn about yourself from Story-Listening, and inserting it into a predictable script that follows the same structure as any of the greatest stories ever told.

(3). Story-Practicing

The story you design for your future has to be powerful enough to convince and mobilize your internal, automatic powers to aid you toward your goals. These powers, largely held in your unconscious mind, are at your command, if only you have the right story and know how to 'sell' it to yourself in the pursuit of your goals. In the end, the key to creating success starts with knowing your past story, designing a future success story, and 'practicing' it over and over until it becomes the unconscious, automatic fuel and power behind your future success.

There are four aspects to practicing and perfecting your success story, all of which are determined through the Story-Listening and Story-Writing processes:

- Self-Story

- Goals

- Minimize weaknesses

- Maximize strengths

The first step involves selling yourself the self-story you created in the Story-Writing process. The next step involves setting and striving toward specific, measurable goals. The third and fourth steps involve maximizing your strengths and minimizing your weaknesses. Together, these actions form a repetitive, ongoing process called 'LeaderPractice' – a disciplined development approach for creating success habits that will take you toward your goals.

This Book Is Organized Around Your Story

Throughout this book, you will be asked to respond to workbook-style questions so that you can create your own answers and populate the various elements of your story. The story of you is a less prescriptive, more discovery-based approach to personal and leadership development, for in the end, your story is a unique journey, of which *you* are by far the most authentic author.

There are five sections in this book, organized around the three levels of activity and the twelve dimensions involved in creating the story of you. The first section introduces the concepts and science behind the Story Of You process. The following three sections describe Story-Listening, Story-Writing, and Story-Practicing, and the fifth section provides a Story Workbook with some rudimentary tools and assessments to get you started on the journey to creating your own success story.

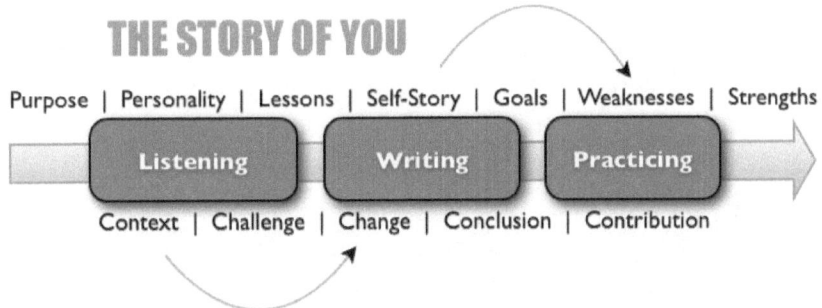

1. **The Story of You:** (where we will discuss all the foundational concepts that power this book, such as story as personal influence, the power of the unconscious mind, and practice as a means of accelerating change).

2. **Story-Listening:** (where we will cover the dimensions of purpose, personality, and lessons).

3. **Story-Writing:** (where we will walk through the framework for creating your story: context, challenge, change, conclusion, and contribution).

4. **Story-Practicing:** (where we will describe the process of LeaderPractice, which involves developing your self-story, pursuing goals, minimizing weaknesses, and maximizing strengths).

5. **The Story Workbook:** (where we will summarize the story-making process and guide you through a structured process for creating the story of you).

When most people think of 'story' they think of story-*telling* – which is what you do to provide a narrative to others after events are over. The idea behind *The Story Of You* is story-*making* – purposefully planning and implementing your own leadership story – while you're still living it. This process involves the juxtaposition of your story assessment dimensions against the way great stories are built, i.e. storyboarding *you* into the five acts of your own evolving story.

Here are your basic takeaways from this book. You'll learn to:

1. Uncover your life's true purpose and passion.

2. 'LeaderPractice' your way to lasting success.

3. Unleash your full potential for high performance at work.

I encourage you to use this book like a reference manual as you begin designing your future. Read it once through, listen to the internet-downloadable audio and music, do the exercises in the workbook sections, and then revisit each section over time as you implement your own growth and development experience.

The three self-leadership skills of Story-Listening, Story-Writing, and Story-Practicing must work together in synergy. You must also work diligently through each of the five acts of your story. You can't implement the process partially. You've got to go all the way, building upon each stage with the rewards and learning you acquire from previous steps.

I share these ideas with you, not from the perceived credibility of vast amounts of external wealth and worldly trappings – that's irrelevant. My experience comes from understanding my own story, clarifying my purpose, designing my future, and finally, choosing to live my dreams – and my message to you is this: you can do it too!

I am honored to begin this journey with you. Sit back, and let's start listening to the story of you …

THE STORY OF YOU

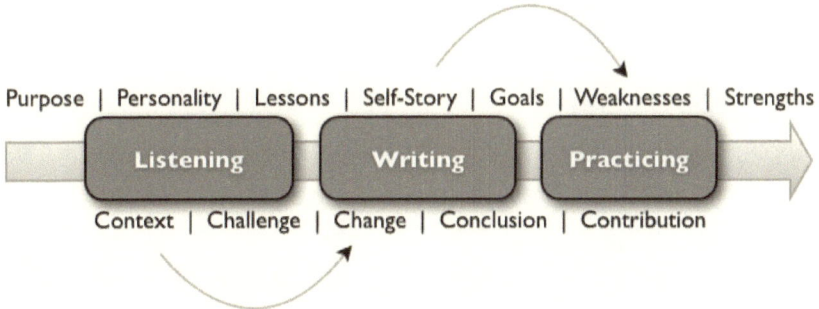

Purpose | Personality | Lessons | Self-Story | Goals | Weaknesses | Strengths

Listening   Writing   Practicing

Context | Challenge | Change | Conclusion | Contribution

Before you can create personal success or lead others to great achievements, you must first lead yourself. This concept – self-leadership – requires that you become crystal clear about your own life's purpose. To do this, you'll need a convincing 'self-story', which will go a long way to help your unconscious powers come alive in the service of your goals. In this section, we'll explore the following:

1. The power of story.

2. *LeaderPractice*: the science of change.

3. The paradox of your 'two minds'.

4. How to *make* the story of you.

Over the course of this section, we'll discuss the foundational concepts and power behind your self-story, and how you can use it to influence and lead yourself to the success you desire.

2.

The Power Of Story

Story is the vessel of influence.
— *PELE RAYMOND UGBOAJAH, PHD.*

The year was 1967, and as bombs flew back and forth, exploding across a crimson, war-torn Nigerian sky, men, women, and children were dying everywhere from wounds, starvation, and disease. Igbo villages had become refugee camps for thousands of families fleeing the encroachment of the Nigeria-Biafra civil war. At the time, I was a refugee child under the protection of my mother and grandparents. I was only two years old, hungry, wearing neither clothes nor shoes, but I was about to receive the most important gift of my life. My name.

Let me tell you the parable of the storyteller, a true story about how I got my name.

The Nigerian civil war had already been raging for several months, resulting in the death of millions. To understand the scale and nature of this conflict, picture in your mind's eye the more recent civil wars of Darfur, Rwanda, or Liberia. It was terrible! You may have seen television footage of young African children with large eyes, even larger, malnourished stomachs, and flies buzzing around their mouths. I was one of those children.

Then one day, a miraculous thing happened. Out of the blue, in the midst of carnage, devastation, and death, a story began to make its way around the war-ravaged country: Pelè, the greatest soccer player on earth, had announced a desire to visit Nigeria for an exhibition soccer match.

In the middle of a civil war!

The story of Pelè's choice to play in Nigeria became so ubiquitous that it wielded a power of its own. It grew through word of mouth from a simple headline in all the newspapers to a parable of mythical proportions across the entire country. Now, if you know much about soccer, you'd understand why Nigerians were so excited that the great Pelè had chosen to play in their country. But no one could have predicted what would happen next.

After deliberations at the highest levels of power, the two governments of Nigeria and Biafra mutually agreed to a forty-eight-hour cease-fire. They stopped the entire war so that soldiers and civilians alike could travel peacefully to the capital city of Lagos and watch Pelè play soccer.

Now *that's* influence!

Here's a question for you. Do you know of any single person, living or dead, who could wield so much influence that two warring nations would stop their bloody conflict for two days? I certainly don't, and neither do any of the people I've ever asked in my seminars. And that was how I got my name. My late father was in the United States at the time, working on his doctorate degree at the University of Minnesota. He was so excited that he telegraphed a message home to my relatives saying that henceforth, my name would become *Pelè*.

Here's how Henry Kissinger told the story of Pelè for TIME magazine's '100 Most Important People of the Century' (Time, 1999):

He was born across the mountains from the great coastal cities of Brazil, in the impoverished town of Tres Coracoes. Nicknamed Dico by his family, he was called Pelè by soccer friends, a word whose origins escape him. Dico shined shoes until he was discovered at the age of 11 by one of the country's premier players, Waldemar de Brito. Four years later, De Brito brought Pelè to Sao Paulo and declared to the disbelieving directors of the professional team in Santos, "This boy will be the greatest soccer player in the world." He was quickly legend. By the next season, he was the top scorer in his league. As the Times of London would later say, "How do you spell Pelé? G-O-D." He has been known to stop war: both sides in Nigeria's civil war called a 48-hour cease-fire in 1967 so Pelè could play an exhibition match in the capital of Lagos.

Like so many people all over the world, my father believed that Pelè had single-handedly stopped the war, and in keeping with Igbo tradition, he simply wanted his son to inherit by association the same traits that had produced such powerful influence.

But my father and the world were mistaken.

It wasn't Pelè the soccer player who stopped that war. It wasn't the *man* who wielded such influence. It was his *story*. Pelè may have been a great soccer player, but without knowing it, he was also an incredible *storyteller!* It was his story that stopped the Nigerian civil war for forty-eight hours.

So what exactly *was* Pelè's story? What was it that made his story so powerful to all these people?

Pelè's story was a vision of endless possibility, a celebration of victory over hopelessness. Imagine a young Brazilian boy, born into poverty, who found a way to climb out of his surroundings through sheer determination. Imagine that this young shoe-shiner literally *practiced* his way to success, and thus became the greatest soccer player, not only of his generation, but also of all time. That was the story that Nigerians heard. It was a story of hope. Pelè's story was evidence that *anything* is possible, not only for Pelè, but also in the lives of everyday people.

That is the parable of the storyteller.

Great stories inspire great action.

Story As Leadership Influence

Throughout the ages, 'story' has been the central communication form that humankind has used to pass on values, ideas, hopes, and fears. It has been used to promote everything from order and balance, to chaos and propaganda. Its use and application has been omnipresent – from electing Presidents to comforting children – but most of all, it has remained one of the most powerful tools of leadership and influence that our human species has at its disposal.

If you want to influence and motivate people, don't offer a list of facts – tell a great story.

Think of the story of Jesus – from his birth to a virgin mother, to his death at the hands of his persecutors. Think of how the story of his sacrifice has endured over the last two thousand years, literally changing the world.

Think of Mandela, whose twenty-seven years of wrongful imprisonment created a narrative so powerful, a myth of sacrifice so inspiring, that it led to the overthrow of Apartheid and propelled him to become South Africa's first black president.

Think of Martin Luther King, whose assassination turned him into a martyr – the ultimate symbol of sacrifice for a worthy cause. Think of how his life's narrative, "I have a dream," ultimately changed America, and over time, led to an environment in which Barack Obama could flourish and become president of the United States.

> In leadership, message vastly outperforms the messenger, and story is infinitely more powerful than the storyteller.

What's really happening behind the scenes is that story wields an almost transcendent power in the human mind. Research shows that unlike when we listen to logic and hard facts, something trancelike happens in our minds when we hear the words "once upon a time." It's as if we are instantly transported to whatever mythical place and time is being described in the story we're listening to, and we feel a deep, emotional, empathetic connection to whatever point the story is making. The connection we feel takes on a life of its own, and spurs us to action. Story, when told with power and conviction, becomes one of our most powerful tools for inspiration, influence, and persuasion.

Story As Personal Influence

So far, we've been discussing leadership storytelling – the kind of influence that is achieved through a story one tells *others*.

But what about the stories we tell ourselves?

Can the quality of our *self-story* influence the quality of our actions? Can a story we tell ourselves be so influential and powerful that we end up marshalling our own strengths, both conscious and unconscious, to the degree that we motivate ourselves to exceed our own expectations? Could a great story we tell ourselves help us achieve levels of leadership, performance, and success that we otherwise would not have ever reached?

Based on an extensive review of available research in neuroscience, positive psychology, and narrative influence, the answer is a resounding "yes!"

We can actually *enroll* reservoirs of strength in our own minds to aid us in achieving our goals, surpassing even our own expectations. But this is only possible if we learn to maximize the quality and urgency in the stories we tell our selves.

> Your level of success is tied to the quality of your **Self-Story** – the story you tell about yourself – to yourself.

What is your self-story? Have you fully explored the dormant power that exists in your already-lived life?

The story within you can move mountains if you pay close attention to it and apply its lessons with unshakable faith. The better the story you uncover and tell, the better you'll be able to convince yourself of a clear path forward. Have no fear, for you too can create a compelling story! Read on, and I'll teach you how. In the end, what holds most of us back are not a lack of ambition and desire, it is just that we haven't yet created and told our own story convincingly – to ourselves.

The Wrong Story Can Destroy Your Destiny

The flip side to the positive power of a convincing self-story is when you have the *wrong* story working in your life. It is very important to be careful what you allow others to tell you about yourself. But even more important is to beware of what story you tell yourself.

Stories are powerful, and the wrong story, if allowed to be the driver of your life's values and actions, can be absolutely devastating. The most challenging thing about the stories we tell ourselves is that we are not always aware of them. Some of the most dangerous self-stories are *hidden*.

One of the most debilitating stories in my life started when I was in my teens. In secondary school, I was a model student – straight A's, the most gifted artist, musician, and storyteller. One day, someone I considered one of my very best friends sat me down and told me something that inadvertently powered my life for far too many years. He was a sharp young man, very energetic, with a penchant for saying things as he saw them. I respected his opinion.

On that fateful day, he said to me, almost jokingly:

"Pelè, you'll never make any money in your life because you're far too talented!" Shocked, I asked him to explain.

"People like you go on to become professors and geniuses, but it's people like me who make all the money."

I was devastated. I wanted to make money, just like everyone else. Why had he singled me out, using my strengths against me in such a cruel manner? I didn't respond much to his statement that day, but internally, I swore to prove him wrong. From that day onward, the hidden self-story I told myself was this:

"He is wrong about me! I must do all I can to be wealthy, just like everyone else, and I'll do that by pushing my innate talents to the background and returning to them only after I've made my fortune."

That was the most destructive story I've ever had in my life. That self-story led me to focus on all the wrong things, and it cost me many years of wasted time. Gladly, I've since dropped that script and replaced it with a more purposeful one.

> **What hidden self-stories are you telling yourself?**

Les Brown, a cherished friend and mentor of mine, once said: "don't let someone else's opinion of you become your reality!" Negative stories have to be the biggest distraction to success in our lives. Like a moth to a flame, the human mind seems to seek out negative information, and over-compensates for it. Because of this, many of us have a very low immunity to negative attacks from both outside and within. Negative self-talk can therefore set you back so much more quickly and effectively than positive self-talk can prop you back up. For every one negative story you tell yourself, you'll need twelve positive ones just to counterbalance it and bring you back onto your correct path.

Be careful whom and what you allow into your mind. Most importantly, be careful what story *you* tell yourself!

Lasting Success Starts With The Question 'Why'

I once had the privilege of meeting Dr. Benjamin Kojo Taylor, an incredibly successful entrepreneur with an even more fascinating story. Dr. Taylor was born in Ghana, and moved to the United States to pursue a higher education. From his humble West African beginnings, he founded and built a $70 million dollar technology services company with offices in 15 US cities, and was listed twice in the INC. 500 as one of the fastest growing private companies in America. He later sold the company to Executrain, publishers of the famous "Dummies" training books series.

When I met Dr. Taylor, he was speaking at a fundraiser for his new venture, which this time, was focused on his lifelong passion and dream of giving back to his native homeland, Africa. His new company, MicroClinics, provides hospitals and medical services to impoverished rural African societies. During his speech, he told a simple story about the reason why he would leave all of his American success to pursue the vision of bringing affordable healthcare to impoverished African areas.

His question was this: "why do millions of young African children have to die each year from malaria, a disease that is almost 100% curable?"

Having been born in Africa, and having experienced the poverty and hopelessness first hand, this question was so powerful for him that it justified whatever sacrifices he would be required to make. His question 'why' drove the creation and implementation of his powerful new success story. His answer to that question became his life's new sense of urgency, business case, and driving purpose.

Armed with such a meaningful purpose, nothing could hold him back, not even the promise of continued financial prowess in America.

> **Why do you do what you do?**

Lead Yourself With A Compelling Self-Story

A myriad of leadership books and research articles have been written on the subjects of motivation and change, for both individuals and organizations. Their findings are applicable to the practice of self-leadership, except that in this case, you are both the follower and the leader. Most of the available research on change and motivation shows that the very first steps to any new, envisioned path to success involves creating a compelling business case. In my view, all of the discoveries and suggestions in the literature can be summed up with the following statement:

Lasting success begins when you develop a strong sense of urgency and a clarified purpose, both of which come from your answer to the simple question: *"why?"*

Why am I doing this?

People don't begin or endure through the process of change unless they are irrefutably sure of their answer to the question "why?" Why must I change? Why must I take on this or that task? Why are we doing what we are doing? Most organizational and personal change projects fail for the simple reason that people haven't established – upfront – a strong enough motivation, business case, or buy-in for whatever task must be done in the future.

The same rule applies to you. If you are not convinced, in both mind and spirit, of the reason why you should do one thing or the other with your life, you just won't do it. You'll procrastinate, won't be motivated or passionate about it, and the moment difficulties arrive at your doorstep, you'll be swayed to change course, which will probably bring you right back to where you started.

The first, and arguably most important thing you can do to create lasting self-leadership and success is to start by answering the question 'why', and then embedding that into the story you tell yourself everyday.

Whether your answer is positive, negative, or a combination of the two, it must create a strong sense of urgency within you. The Pavlovian point of view would suggest that positive answers help to push us toward some form of pleasure, while negative answers will help take us away from some form of pain. Positive answers could be: "I'll have more time for my family," or "I'll be able to give back to my hometown." Negative answers could be: "I never want to be fired again," or "I won't let my team fail." Either way, you must find out and remind yourself constantly what *you* really care about. Lasting success depends on the sense of urgency you embed into your self-story.

Story is one of the most powerful influence technologies that humankind possesses. Tell a great story, and you can change the world. Pelè's story stopped an African civil war. Mandela's story stopped Apartheid. Martin Luther King's story paved the way for America to elect its first African American president.

Leaders everywhere use story – narrative as influence – to inspire, motivate, and transform others into highly productive, successful followers. If great stories are so influential when directed at others, what about your own self-story, if it were powerfully constructed, and directed at you? The same rules of influence, motivation, and inspiration to action that apply when a great story is told to others are applicable when you tell your own mind a great story.

This is at the heart of self-leadership. By understanding, creating, and delivering a powerful, influential narrative to yourself, you can achieve great things, and exceed even your own expectations of success.

> **Success means finding out what you really care about – and then doing it.**

What is YOUR story? Imagine what YOUR story would be if told by others. Write down in one paragraph, 'the story of you' as you know it today.

_____

_____

_____

_____

_____

What is your answer to the question of 'why' you do what you do today?

_____

_____

_____

_____

Write down the 3 top points you learned from this chapter.

_____

_____

_____

So far, we've discussed the power of strategic, influential storytelling, not only with respect to leaders and followers, but also, and more importantly, with respect to leading yourself. Your audience – the internal one in your own mind – will only be motivated to work for you if your story's message and delivery are influential and compelling.

We've also talked about making sure you're telling yourself the right stories. Your mind is not partial to positive stories; negative stories will work on you just fine, and are probably even more influential if you allow them into your value system.

If you want to motivate yourself to positive action, you must research, create, and tell yourself a positive, convincing self-story. The more true and compelling the story, the more powerful the change.

Later on, we'll talk about how to create this influential self-story. For now, let's take a closer look at the science behind how you can use that story – once it is ready – to *power* your future success.

3.

LeaderPractice:
The Science Of Change

Life is like riding a bicycle.
– ALBERT EINSTEIN

It was the summer of 2007, and I was teaching one of my young daughters how to ride her first bicycle. For a while she had been using her training wheels, and on this particular day, she insisted on taking them off. After some negotiation, we finally decided to take them off, and we jumped into our new adventure together with faith and conviction.

Our task was not easy – we knew it involved helping her create skills she had never possessed before. We were trying to produce lasting change, and I must say that I learned more about how to create success from something she said to me than from most of the books I've ever read on the subject.

What I learned is something I now call 'LeaderPractice'.

Let me explain.

As we embarked on this new journey without training wheels, I remember noticing how hard she tried, and how many times she fell off her bike – painfully – over and over again. I realized that what was really going on here was that her conscious mind wanted this to work out really badly, but she hadn't yet developed the ability to ride her bike 'unconsciously' – or in other words, without consciously thinking about it. Whatever neurons in her brain were supposed to automate the various instructions and tasks involved in riding a bicycle hadn't yet started firing off.

It was agonizing to watch her strain her face as she tried to *think* harder to get it done, and yet, her muscles and her body just weren't responding. I remember thinking, *wouldn't it be great if she could just hit a button in her brain that would put her on automatic cruise control* – a kind of 'autopilot' button in her mind?

One particular day, with tears in her eyes, she came over to me and said, "Daddy, I just can't do this!"

I held her close and whispered in her ear. "Yes, you can," and sent her back for some more practice.

She tried again and again, going over the same fundamentals I had been teaching her, and after another series of failures, we finally called it a day.

But what neither of us realized was that we had just experienced her last bike-riding failure ever.

The very next day, we went out to ride again, and an amazing thing happened. Without warning, she soared away from my protective grip and rode the bicycle several yards on her own. Surprised, she tried it again, and astonished us both by going even further.

Somehow that cruise control button in her mind had been hit! My daughter had just learned how to ride a bicycle!

What *changed* overnight? What threshold was crossed so that she was suddenly able to do something she was unable to do the previous day? What was the biology behind that change? Was it a sudden change, or had it been developing all along, and we just weren't aware of it? I stopped her and asked her what she had done differently, and here's what she told me:

"I don't know what I did. All of a sudden, I was able to do it without thinking about it!"

Without *thinking* about it!

Her answer – that simple statement – taught me more about how to create lasting change than all the books I've ever read on the subject. What she had done was basically this: through repetition and practice, she had literally transferred her goal, and the various tasks of riding a bicycle, from her *conscious* mind, into her *unconscious* mind. Only then could she achieve so much automatically and concurrently – balance, force, and direction – all without ever being aware of it. Only then was she able to achieve lasting change, and do so much more than she was capable of doing a day earlier. I learned that day that the key to lasting change was to be found in this kind of conscious-to-unconscious transfer process.

Eureka!

Habit Formation – The Key To Lasting Change

It occurred to me that even though we saw a change in my daughter's riding skills overnight, it had actually taken a lot of repetition and practice before the actual effect could be seen. Instead of struggling to ride her bicycle consciously, she was now riding her bike 'unconsciously', meaning that a part of her mind had taken over all the duties of balance and self-propulsion without her awareness of it. (The word 'unconscious' doesn't mean you've literally passed out. It just refers to a part of your mind that is working without your conscious awareness of it).

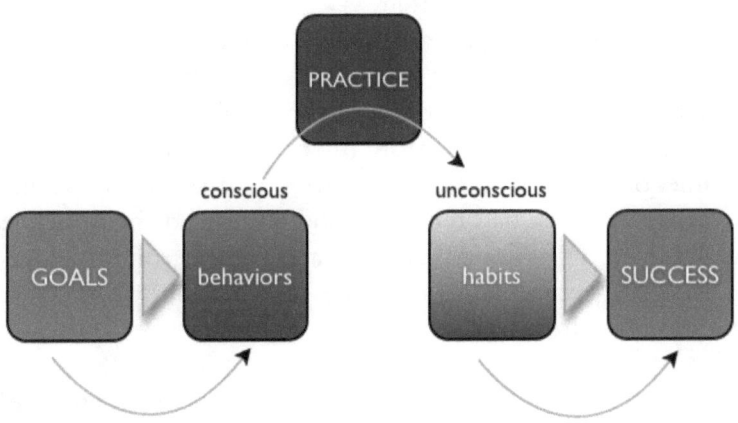

What she had created in her mind was a new set of automatic, neural pathways – habits – that could work *for* her, without her awareness of it. She broke down complex goals into constituent behaviors, and practiced those behaviors until they become habits, which eventually supported her success.

This is called Leader*Practice,* a behavioral and skill development process for creating lasting habits in the more powerful, automatic, unconscious mind.

You Can't Learn To Play Soccer At A Seminar

Whenever I conduct a leadership seminar, I start with a short parable about how people learn. I call it; "You can't learn to play soccer at a seminar."

There were once two leaders who attended one of my sales leadership seminars. One was extremely fast, and could understand things in one sitting. The other wasn't so fast at grasping the concepts, and would always ask questions to clarify his understanding. At the end of the seminar, both came up to me and thanked me for my time. They both filled out and signed a document that I requested from them, which promised that they would implement what they had learned, and in a year, it was my job to call them and ask after their progress.

I called them both back a year later and here were the results: the fast gentleman had never once looked at the training information since the day we last met a year prior. He had built no skills, and had just been laid off a few weeks before my call. The other gentleman had become one of the strongest leaders in their business unit because, every week, he had rehearsed and reinforced the principles I had taught them. His sales conversion rates were astronomical, and he had become a genuine rising star in his organization.

What was the difference?

Practice.

When asked how he became such a fantastic soccer legend, Pelè of Brazil simply answered: "Practice is *everything!*" You could see he meant it, because he would spend hours, days, and weeks practicing his famous dribbles and kicks. One of his most famous feats, the *bicycle kick*, earned him far-reaching credibility as the world's top soccer player of all time. And he credits everything to one simple concept: practice. When you apply repetitive development processes to leadership skills and behavior, and when you commit yourself to getting out and practicing what you learn, I call it LeaderPractice – because you can't learn to play soccer at a seminar.

**You Can't Learn to Play
Soccer at a Seminar™**

Like soccer – or any other game – if you want to excel, you actually have to go out onto the field and practice. At some point, what was once conscious effort will transfer into unconscious action, and you'll find yourself achieving great things beyond your current expectations. You will watch yourself soar, and it'll be just like hitting a cruise control button in your life.

Consider the 70-20-10 rule, which says that people learn best through experience – *practicing* – what they learn. The same concept works when it comes to self-leadership. Your mind will learn best how to automatically help reach your goals if you practice the story you design for how you'll get there.

> ### The 70:20:10 Rule:
> Research shows that people learn primarily through practice.
>
> 70% of learning comes from 'doing', 20% comes from people around you, and 10% comes from formal training in a classroom environment.

Intuitively, we all know that practice makes one better at things, yet most organizations invest 80% of their training into formal learning, where the least learning takes place (Jennings, 2007). Obviously, there is a huge chasm between knowing something and doing it – which is why so many people know what they need to do, but struggle to execute. To bridge the gap between knowing and doing, you need LeaderPractice, a disciplined process for developing success habits through the simple, and proven concept of practice.

When you apply the principles of practice to leadership tasks, to selling your story to yourself, and to achieving whatever goals you set for yourself, you will see daily, gradual improvements until you are able to form whatever habits you seek. And one of the benefits of pushing tasks from the conscious to the unconscious mind is that you don't have to think about them any more. They become habits that are automatic and *permanent*.

> ### Practice doesn't only make perfect.
> ### Practice makes permanent.

I saw this play out firsthand when I enrolled for my first-ever Toastmasters speaking competition. I had never spoken in a competition before, but once I learned the basics, I took it upon myself to practice day and night, until I was able to rehearse entire speeches and deliver them flawlessly. As a result of this LeaderPractice, I went from novice to the District 6 Toastmasters Champion of Public Speaking in a matter of months. And the only reason I became proficient at speaking in public was because speaking was no longer a conscious process for me. I had transferred it to my unconscious mind.

Just like my daughter did with her bike.

I've learned over the years that knowing *why* certain principles work – not just the fact that they do – is very helpful if you want to implement them successfully.

So, what exactly is the power behind the principle of LeaderPractice? How is it that these kinds of potent habits are formed in the mind? How is it that your story can be 'sold' to your unconscious powers so that they can carry you to great achievements?

Let's explore that.

4.

The Paradox Of Your Two Minds

*"If the desire to get somewhere is strong enough in a person, his whole being,
conscious and unconscious, is always at work, looking for and devising means to
get to the goal"*
– FREDERICK PHILIP GROVE

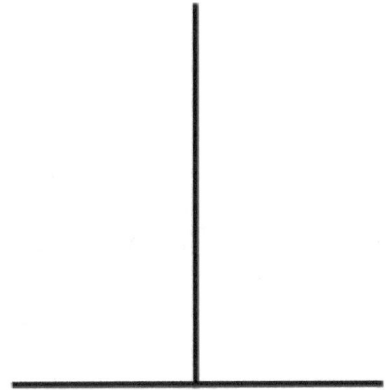

Which of the two lines in this diagram would you say is longer: the
horizontal, or the vertical? Check one box:

☐ Horizontal Line
☐ Vertical Line

If you're like most people, (who haven't seen this exercise), you probably picked the vertical line as the longer of the two lines.

And if you did, you were wrong!

Both lines are exactly the same length: two inches. (Grab a ruler and confirm their lengths for yourself). Here are the same two lines, this time, placed together horizontally:

See the difference? When the two lines are parallel, they appear to be the same exact length – two inches. However, when one is vertical, it appears longer.

Why does this happen?

Here's why. Literally speaking, your eyes were playing tricks on you!

Or better stated, your more powerful unconscious mind was doing what it does best: automatically 'filling in the gaps' to keep you safe, and to do this, it had to overpower your conscious mind.

This particular experiment, (the horizontal-vertical illusion) was made popular in 1858 by the German psychologist Wilhelm (Max) Wundt (Colman, 2001). No one has proven conclusively why this illusion occurs, but the scientific community has long been intrigued by what it demonstrates – the brain's automatic tendency to respond to inputs by 'filling in the blanks'.

Some researchers have hypothesized that this automatic – *unconscious* – brain mechanism is an evolutionary process that was valuable for human survival. As a result of evolving in the outdoors, human beings learned to associate things that are vertical with recession into the horizon. The effect is that your mind will still automatically race to determine that a vertical line seems 'longer' – no matter how hard you *consciously* try to readjust or justify what you see!

The Power of Your Unconscious Mind

You may have heard the urban myth that we consciously use only 10% of our minds at any given time. The other 90% – the unconscious mind – is supposedly doing most of the work for us, without our awareness. While this myth has been proven false by over 150 years of neuropsychological research, it still points to a certain reality: scientists continue to discover new ways of showing us that people may not be using the mind to its fullest capacity.

For example, in 2006, social scientists Ap Dijksterhuis and Loran Nordgren laid out a theory of human thought called the unconscious-thought theory (UTT), which makes the point that the unconscious mind is capable of processing much more information and arriving at higher quality *decisions* than the conscious mind (Dijksterhuis & Nordgren, 2006).

They carried out experiments to test which of these two minds (unconscious or conscious) could handle increasing complexity better. They asked people to choose between four apartments with twelve features each, and increased the complexity along the way. As the complexity of the problem increased, they found that conscious thought broke down, while the unconscious continued to high quality decisions. Following is the diagram and summary of their findings:

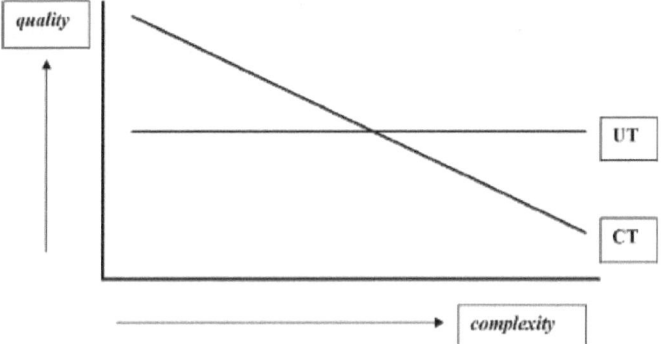

Fig. 1. The relation between the quality and complexity of a decision, as predicted by unconscious-thought theory. For conscious thought (CT), quality varies as a function of complexity, whereas for unconscious thought (UT), it does not.

This much is true: your unconscious mind is working for you all the time, whether you know it or not. If you've ever had to make a difficult decision, and then decided to 'sleep on it', only to wake up or be in the shower a few days later and the solution pops into your brain – seemingly from nowhere – you were experiencing the power of the unconscious mind. Think of what it takes to type a paper or give a speech. Your conscious mind controls the things you want to communicate, but it is your vastly more powerful unconscious mind that is processing all the functional actions, controlling your fingers as they type the words, or shaping your mouth and tongue appropriately to produce your vocalizations.

That powerful unconscious mind is where my daughter's automatic bicycle-riding skills now reside. It is also the audience for your self-story. The better you are at motivating your unconscious mind, the better you'll be at harnessing it – as powerful as it is – in the service of your goals.

What if we could push the goals and tasks we struggle with at a conscious level, down to the unconscious mind? What if we could learn to harness that automatic, unconscious power? How far could we go?

> The unconscious mind of man sees correctly, even when conscious reason is blind and impotent.
>
> – Carl Jung

Two Minds Are Better Than One

I once took my children to a circus at the Target Center in downtown Minneapolis. While there, we saw the most amazing feats and stunts – performed by animals. We saw elephants standing on their two front feet, and tigers jumping through fire hoops. It was mesmerizing! But most of all, I was captivated by how the trainers fearlessly and elegantly interacted with their tigers, horses and elephants – animals so much more powerful than they – yet dutifully enrolled in their service. Individually the two were impressive, but working together in harmony, they were fascinating!

Watching them, I couldn't help but be drawn to the powerful metaphor inherent in their interaction. Your unconscious mind is the elephant, and you are the trainer. The elephant is much more physically powerful than the trainer, but with skill, practice and patience, the trainer can enroll the elephant in her service. Both working together will create feats that are far superior than they could ever do individually.

> **Together, your 'two minds' can do great things.**

There have been many great metaphors used to explain how the conscious and unconscious minds work together. One of the most popular analogies is the iceberg metaphor.

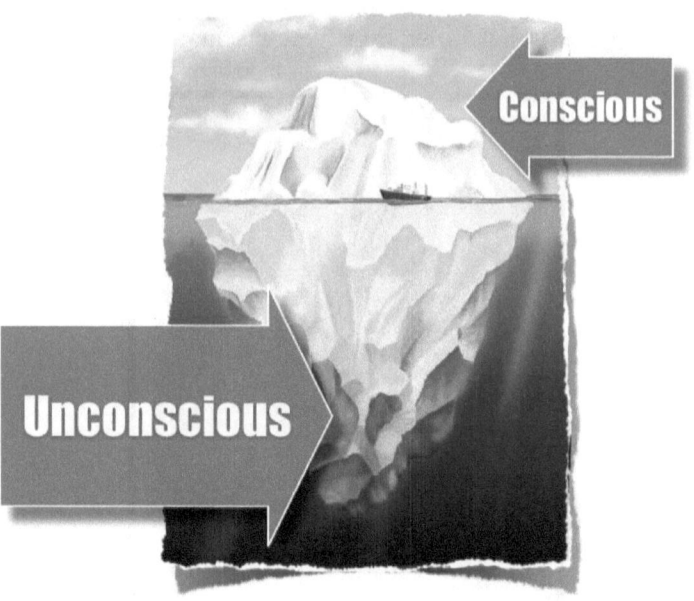

The mind is like an iceberg, you only see the tip of it, (the conscious mind), whereas most of the horsepower is actually happening in the portion of the iceberg which we don't see below the water (the unconscious mind). Think of the conscious mind as the part of our minds that we are 'aware' of while it is thinking. The unconscious mind is also 'thinking' at all times, but we are just not aware of it. It just works automatically in the background.

Another metaphor – my personal favorite – comes from The Buddha, and was made popular by Jonathan Haidt in his book, *The Happiness Hypothesis*:

> *"In days gone by this mind of mine used to stray wherever selfish desire or lust or pleasure would lead it. Today this mind does not stray and is under the harmony of control, even as a wild elephant is controlled by the trainer"* (Haidt, 2006).

The elephant is the powerful unconscious mind, and the rider, like the trainer in the circus, is the conscious mind. When they work together, the results are fascinating. The better the trainer is at working with, and inspiring the elephant to controlled action, the better the performance will be.

Our lives work the same way. The key to achieving great success in life and at work is to enroll your two minds in a coordinated effort toward achieving your goals.

According to what social psychologists now know about the goal-directed inclination of the paired, conscious/unconscious brain, it turns out that two minds are indeed better than one.

Purpose: How To Put Your Two Minds To Work

The unconscious mind is a very 'goal-directed' part of the human brain. It needs to be fed the right *purpose* in order for it to work in our favor. The illusion at the beginning of this chapter was designed to help you experience the silent vigor with which your all-powerful unconscious mind will pursue a goal – even one that has been set for it over years of evolution. In this case, your unconscious mind 'filled in the blanks' to create the illusion that a vertical line was longer than a horizontal one.

What one has to do is learn to 'teach' the unconscious mind what goals are most important. In a sense, one has to 'tame' the unconscious mind so that it will work *for* us, not against us.

Fortunately, the unconscious mind's 'goal-orientation' is impartial. It will carry out whatever instructions it is fed. To demonstrate this impartial aptitude, Dr. Joseph Disperna showed in MRI experiments that the same parts of the brain light up when a person is looking at an object or *imagining* it (Arntz et al., 2004). Your unconscious mind does not distinguish between the real and the imagined, which means that you have the power to imagine and create whatever intentions you desire, and enroll your two minds in the service of those goals.

> You have the power to CREATE your success story,
> and then ENROLL your unconscious mind in the
> service of that story.

Consider this quote from Dr. Maxwell Maltz, about the goal-oriented tendency of the unconscious mind:

> *Insofar as function is concerned, the brain and nervous system constitute a marvelous and complex "goal-striving mechanism," a sort of built-in automatic guidance system which works for you as a "success mechanism," or against you as a "failure mechanism," depending on how "YOU," the operator, operate it and the goals you set for it (Maltz, 1960).*

The need for creating and maintaining a positive and effective 'self-image' is well known in positive psychology. What is not often discussed is how this new self-image is used to support and manifest your goals as your story evolves.

My contribution to this debate is that the self-image, no matter how positive it may be, needs a 'self-story' for inspiration and direction. Creating a 'self-story' is like making a blueprint for what your future success will look like. Your self-story helps you implant a compelling, influential 'success story' into your mind. The more relevant, purposeful, and influential the story you tell yourself, the more inspired and coordinated your two minds will be as they work to manifest your goals.

> **Essentially, you need to become a motivational speaker – a success storyteller – to yourself!**

How Your Story Can Power Your Success

Although wrongly attributed to Goethe, William Hutchinson Murray wrote the following words, in his 1951 book, The Scottish Himalayan Expedition (Lee, 1998). What he describes as 'providence' is interchangeable with the power of your mind:

> *Until one is committed, there is hesitancy, the chance to draw back. Concerning all acts of initiative (and creation), there is one elementary truth, the ignorance of which kills countless ideas and splendid plans: that the moment one definitely commits oneself, then Providence moves too. All sorts of things occur to help one that would never otherwise have occurred. A whole stream of events issues from the decision, raising in one's favor all manner of unforeseen incidents and meetings and material assistance, which no man could have dreamed would have come his way. Whatever you can do, or dream you can do, begin it. Boldness has genius, power, and magic in it. Begin it now."*

There is nothing as powerful and success-oriented as a made-up mind. Once you clearly discern your purpose from listening to your own story, your conscious mind will form a powerful partnership with your unconscious mind to guide you toward the success you seek.

The particular part of the brain that helps to orchestrate this link has been described as the *reticular activation system* (RAS). You can think of your RAS as the rider on the powerful elephant. In order to explain how the RAS works, let's take a look at a phenomenon in nature that closely resembles it: homing pigeons.

You may have heard of the uncanny ability that homing pigeons have for finding their way home even after being blindfolded and driven miles away from their nesting grounds. Many theories have been proposed over the years to try to explain this phenomenon. Some of the earliest suggestions were that the pigeons rely on magnetic fields in the earth to guide them home.

More recently, researchers point to a heightened awareness that the birds have to certain atmospheric odors and visual landmarks, using these to generate cues for finding their way home. Overall, researchers are beginning to agree that homing pigeons actually navigate and follow location-based cues, much like humans do (BBC, 2004).

The unconscious RAS system in your brain works in a similar way. When you are rock-solid clear on a purpose, a goal, or a vision, the RAS takes over, and increases your sense of awareness regarding certain necessary cues and markers on your way to success. This results in an increased capability to move in the direction of success, and a large amount of the heavy lifting happens entirely in your powerful, unconscious mind.

For example, have you ever bought a car – and after months of planning, saving, and searching, you finally found the right color, trim, and car of your liking, only to find out that after you bought it, you were noticing the same exact car and trim everywhere on the streets? Well, there weren't more cars like yours all of a sudden – it was your sense of awareness that had dramatically increased. Like a homing pigeon, you had become acutely aware of the features you needed that would navigate you to a successful car purchase.

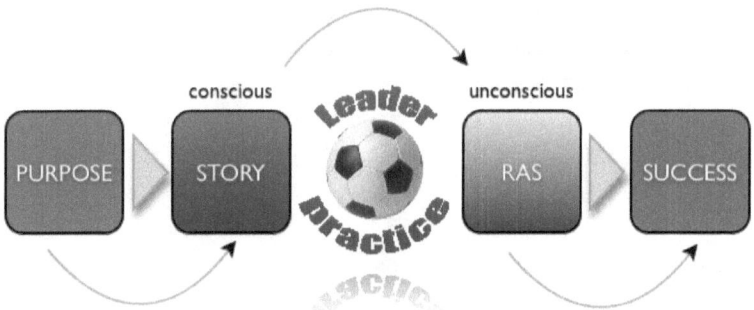

The secret to enrolling your two minds in the service of your goals is by first deciding on a clear purpose and a set of goals. Following that, you create a self-story, and through repetitive visioning and practice methods, (such as LeaderPractice) you can cement the intention for success in your mind by transferring it from conscious thought to unconscious action. Once your reticular activation system (RAS) is programmed with this clear purpose, like the rider, it will push, inspire, and motivate your elephant – the unconscious mind – to action. The powerful elephant will then faithfully and steadily guide you to your goals.

> ### Two MINDS are better than one!

So far, we've covered the concepts and technologies around how your story can be used to influence you personally, and how practice can help you transfer the tasks in that success story into unconscious actions. In much the same way that a child must practice over and over until riding a bike becomes an automatic function, self-leadership involves practicing certain skills over and over until they become 'unconscious'.

LeaderPractice is the process of transferring intentions, goals, and skills from the conscious mind to the infinitely more powerful unconscious mind.

Once your inherently more powerful unconscious mind takes charge of automatic habits, your likelihood of achieving your success story multiplies exponentially.

Now, let's review how to create your success story in the first place. Let's take a look at how to design the story of you.

5.

How To Make The Story Of You

All the world's a stage.
– WILLIAM SHAKESPEARE

Once upon a time, there were two newly appointed leaders. One lived in the valley, and one lived in the mountain. Every two years, the emerging leaders were required to switch places, in order to gain experience in a different leadership environment. On the day of the first switch, the leader from the valley met an old, wise man as he traveled up toward the valley.

Stopping, he asked the old man, "Can you advise me about the people in the mountain?"

"Tell me your story," the old man said. "What did you experience in the valley?"

"Well," said the young man, "I've had the worst experience trying to lead the people in the valley. They were unbelievably unruly and chaotic. How are the people up in the mountain?"

The wise old man looked at the young leader and spoke in a somber voice. "You will find that the people in the mountain are just like the people in the valley."

Unhappily, the young leader marched on, up toward his new leadership role in the mountain.

The next day, the leader in the mountain was making his way down to the valley, and he also noticed the old man sitting by the roadside. He stopped to talk with the old man.

"Can you advise me about the people in the valley?"

"Tell me your story," the old man said. "What did you experience in the mountain?"

"I had an amazing time working with the people in the mountain," he said. "They were courteous, great team players, and we had a blast achieving our goals. How are the people in the valley?"

The wise old man looked at the young leader and spoke in a somber voice: "you will find that the people in the valley are just like the people in the mountain."

Happily, the young leader marched on, down toward his new leadership role in the valley.

> **Success is the product of your self-story.**

Your self-story emanates from your operating paradigm – the lens through which you view your life's events – whether you are aware of it or not. What you believe deep inside will lead to what you do, and will manifest into what you get from life. If you believe you are a success, then you are, and will always be one. If, on the other hand, you believe you are a failure, you will manifest that as well.

Do you know what you believe?

The following are the steps you'll need to uncover your past story, design your future success story, and then practice it to the point of perfection and permanence:

1. Develop a new self-story for yourself.

2. Leverage your purpose, personality, and lessons-learned.

3. Through 'practice', communicate your self-story to yourself

Now, let's take a closer look at these three steps.

Step 1. Develop A Self-Story

When you look at your life as an evolving narrative, you are adopting what I call the *self-story* point-of-view. The self-story point of view requires that you begin to see everything in your past as a collection of personal lessons, which were presented to you as a guide toward something greater, something uniquely yours. The lessons you learn can help you identify your purpose in life, hone in on your strengths, and mitigate your weaknesses so that you can make the right decisions about your future.

In your self-story, you are in control of future outcomes, not only as the hero of the story, but also as the storyteller.

Think of what happens when you visit a doctor. The first thing the doctor will do is examine your medical history through a review of records, discussions, or observations from family members. This process of data gathering helps to put together your *medical* story, which will inform what the doctor prescribes for you going forward. How comfortable would you be if a doctor you just met gave you a prescription without learning anything about you or your medical history? In the eyes of a physician, you are more than a bunch of current symptoms. They use a story point-of-view to gain a more holistic understanding of your medical situation.

> The self-story is a way of looking at your life as though it is an evolving story, in which you are both the hero and the storyteller.

Like the director of a motion picture, you have the power to take a look at the story patterns that have occurred in your life so far, and re-engineer your own successful conclusion. The process of making the new story of you involves *listening* to the past and present, *writing* down new goals and outcomes for the future, and then *practicing* those goals until they become unconscious 'habits'.

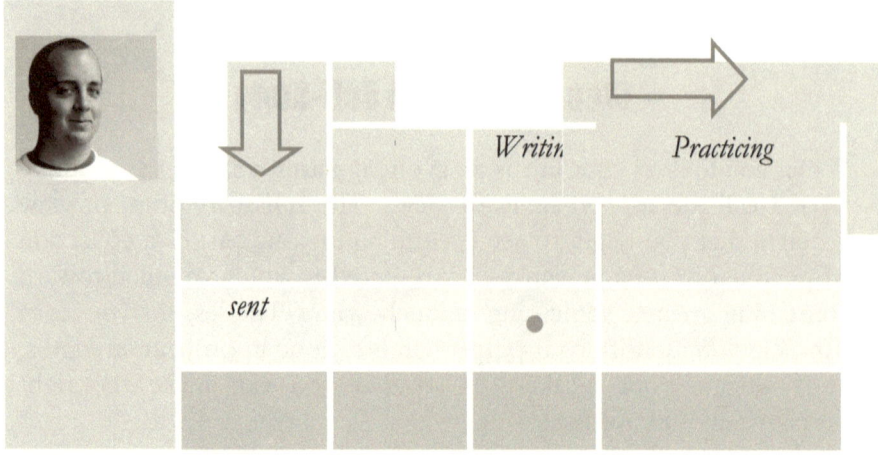

The key to your future success lies in figuring out exactly what your self-story is, where you are in it, and then in making a conscious series of strategic design choices for the rest of it – while you're still living it.

This process is not for the faint of heart! You could compare it to the idea of flying an airplane while assembling its parts. You have to work in real-time. Your life won't *wait* for you to get ready!

The preceding picture is from a popular ad campaign I used as a Director of marketing at EDS. We called the campaign, "Airplane," and the ad was a huge success because it showed prospective customers that they were like an airplane in flight, and had no choice but to work on their challenges now, *while* their core businesses hurried along in real-time.

Like the airplane, your story won't stop for you, or wait for you to get ready. You are building your story already – while you're living it – whether you do so consciously or not. The question is this: will you design it to fit your true specifications for success, or will you leave your life's outcomes to happenstance?

Step 2. Leverage Your Lessons

One of my past coaching clients – a physician – had a recurring challenge that made her feel like a complete failure, making it difficult for her to function at her highest professional potential. Her trigger for this feeling came when she'd hear about old medical school classmates, some of whom had gone on to become renowned in her field. She also felt this way whenever anything reminded her of the decision she made in the past to give up her original dream of becoming a neurosurgeon. When the triggers came, she would be thrown out of control, and would descend into depression and tears. Despite overwhelming evidence that she was a very accomplished emergency room (ER) doctor, she just couldn't get herself to see the success she already had.

You would find her self-viewpoint even more astonishing if you knew some more specifics about her story.

My client is a well-paid physician who works for herself, and thus, controls her own hours. She is beloved and respected by colleagues and patients alike, in particular because of her high-content, detail-oriented, yet loving approach to her work. To anyone who knows her, she is like a walking encyclopedia of medical knowledge, and she does everything she can, (including unorthodox treatments like telling jokes, singing and reading poetry), to put her patients at great ease when she explains things to them. She frequently receives letters of commendation and praise from past patients and hospital administrators, and she is highly sought after for advice by her colleagues and other physician friends.

So what's the problem, you might ask?

The problem is that whenever she is forced to remember the decision she made in her past not to complete her neurosurgery training, she gets into a terrible cycle where she asks herself "what if?" What if I had gone on to be a neurosurgeon? What if I had completed the exams? Wouldn't I be much more successful today? What if? *What if?*

This viewpoint she held – her self-story – was proving to be very debilitating, because she thought about it everyday, and it weighed her down from feeling passionate and positive about her current career. Her prevailing self-story did not inspire her; rather, it drained her of energy. The saddest thing she ever told me was that her only occasional comfort came when she was able to temporarily *forget* about the past.

My advice to her was this: *forgetting the past is not a solution!* Sweeping pain under the rug may put it out of sight, but it's still in the room with you. You have to address the past – head on – and learn something about yourself from it.

You have to search the past for clues and lessons that will help you design the best self-story for your future!

I have since worked with this client to help her go back into the past, come to terms with her lessons, and develop a new, 'self-influential' story for the future. This process has proved very enlightening for her, and has ultimately led her to feel much more personally and professionally fulfilled. But the first step she had to take was to stop seeing her life as a series of events that produced either successes or failures. The first step was to learn to see her life as an evolving, cohesive story, in which there are no successes or failures – only lessons that can be leveraged for future success.

Step 3. Tell Yourself Your New Self-Story

Take a look at the following picture. Have you ever attended a presentation where members of the audience were literally falling asleep during the story? Or better yet, have you ever been the storyteller at one of those presentations? Go ahead, if you have, you can admit it – no one's looking. If so, consider this: how can you ever inspire people to action with a badly constructed, boring, non-influential story?

Think of all these sleeping people as habitants of your own unconscious mind. What must you do to craft and deliver a story they (in your unconscious mind) will respond to?

How will you motivate yourself to action?

Here's another way of asking the same critical question. If you *don't* learn the rules of how to create and tell your future success story, how will you ever live a designed life – and not one ruled by the winds of circumstance?

Making and telling powerful, well-crafted, influential stories about your future success – to yourself – is not that easy. But the good news is that you can *learn* how to do it. One of the major goals of this book is to teach you how to make and tell action-inspiring, influential stories about yourself – to yourself.

> If leadership is about influencing others, then self-leadership is about influencing yourself.

The goal here is that you will become the writer, director, and hero of your own film – the star of your own reality series. Thankfully, there is a method to the madness of creating and delivering great stories – even to yourself.

The first thing you need to learn is the basic structure of *story*. Just as a painter starts with a sketch, and a filmmaker starts with a storyboard, there is a structural framework that can be your starting template for the ultimate design of your future self-story.

That framework is the five 'acts' of your story.

How To Design The Five 'Acts' Of Your Story

Picture in your mind's eye, the greatest adventure movie you've ever watched, and look for patterns as the story evolves. One of my favorites is Mel Gibson's *Braveheart*. Think of how it began; a debilitating difficulty was revealed; the hero, against all odds, discovered his calling and brought about a needed change, saving the day while simultaneously saving his soul.

Consider the patterns of any powerful, inspirational story you've ever read or listened to. My all-time favorite is the epic tale of Jesus. Whatever your beliefs may be, you cannot help but marvel at the timeless beauty and grace of that story – how a carpenter's son grew up amidst a decaying world; was revealed as the chosen one to bring about man's absolution from sin; offered up his own life, the ultimate sacrifice, not for his own gain, but for the salvation of all mankind throughout eternity. What *power*!

Now consider the lives of some of the greatest historical or contemporary leaders in politics or business. Think of people like Nelson Mandela, Martin Luther King, Henry Ford, or Ray Kroc of McDonalds. Again, the patterns are always the same; a *context* is established, a *challenge* appears, a hero brings about *change*, a *conclusion* is reached, and at the end, a *contribution* – a teachable point – is made for all of us to learn from.

I have found that movies, business and political figures' lives, folklore, and myth all use the same structural framework. This is not by accident. It is well known amongst those who study narrative that stories share a universal, predictable pattern. However, these patterns are not just for the big screen, church sermons, fireside gatherings, or famous people and popular books. These patterns are tangible, real narrative phases that are happening in *your* future life and business story – today.

Although 'story' is usually a narrative of *past* events, I found these story patterns, (or acts), to be very useful as a creative framework for guiding the proactive creation of a person's *future* story. By following the same framework, pattern, and rules required for making influential past stories, you can create a powerful, motivational future story for the rest of your life. Let's take a look at this universal pattern of stories, which I call, the Five Acts of story:

> **The Five 'Acts' of Your Story**
> Context
> Challenge
> Change
> Conclusion
> Contribution

When you use the five acts framework as a starting point to design your future, you will gain important insights as you examine each piece of your story. Here are the five acts again, with a quick description of what you'll learn and gain by examining each phase. By understanding these elements in your story, you will be able to construct your profile, explain the present, and begin a proactive process for designing your future.

Story 'Act'	What you learn	What you gain
Context	Who you are	Purpose and Lessons
Challenge	Opportunities	Urgency for change
Change	What you must do	Success Framework
Conclusion	What success is	Your vision of success
Contribution	The point of your story	What you *give* to society

The first step that you must take in order to tap into the inherent truths and power in your story is start with the end in mind.

Then, you must stop and *listen* to your already-lived life story – as if someone else were telling 'the story of you' – to you. Due to the nature of the human narrative process, the story will have a structure that is similar to that of any great story you've ever experienced. As such, it will have the same components we discussed earlier in roughly this order: *context, challenge, change, conclusion*, and *contribution*.

All you have to do next is *write* your future story now, and then get ready to *practice* the behaviors and dimensions you'll highlight along the way, which will lead you to the success you seek. We will cover examples of how to write your self-story in the following section on Story-Writing.

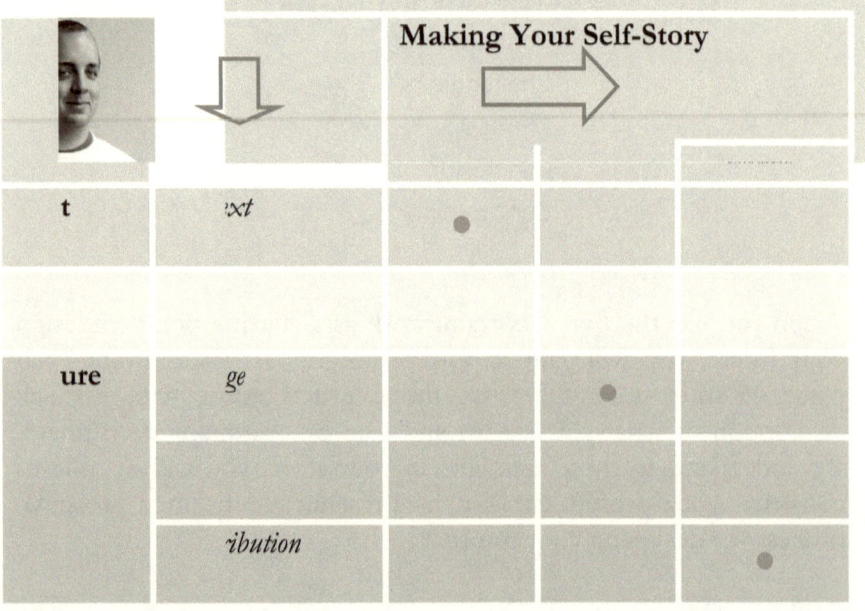

Someday when your life's story is told, it will be explained in this exact same format: a beginning, middle, and an end. You'll be described in terms of your starting context, a set of challenges, some change events, a conclusion, and then, the final contribution of your life – the moral of your story.

There will be much to learn someday about the journey you traveled, and the mountains you conquered. But today, your task is to proactively design that story today, *before* it is over.

STORY-LISTENING

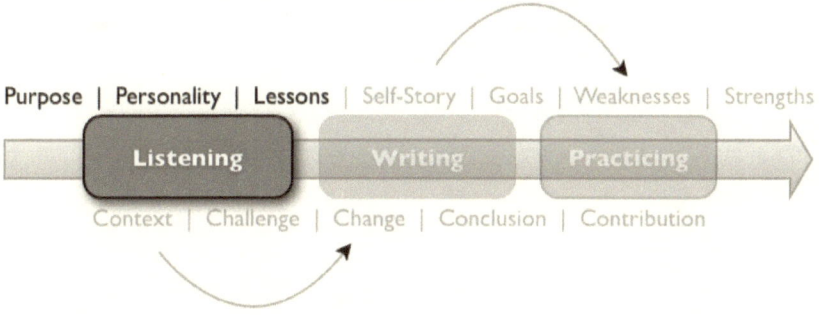

Purpose | Personality | Lessons | Self-Story | Goals | Weaknesses | Strengths

Listening | Writing | Practicing

Context | Challenge | Change | Conclusion | Contribution

So far we've introduced the general concepts, tools, and technologies you'll need for uncovering your self-story, creating a future story, and using that new story to influence yourself toward success. We described three self-leadership skills for achieving this: (1) Story-Listening, (2) Story-Writing, and (3) Story-Practicing. We also talked about LeaderPractice – how to use your story to create lasting change. In the following sections of the book, we'll switch gears and begin the process of actually getting this done. Let's start with **Story-listening**, where you will experience a 'story-assessment' process, involving the following dimensions:

1. Purpose

2. Personality

3. Lessons

By the end of this section, you'll be ready to move to the next skill – Story-writing – where you will use what you learn about yourself to map out a new, successful future story.

6.

Purpose

It is better to lose some of the battles in the struggle for your dreams than to be defeated without ever knowing what you're fighting for.
– PAULO COELHO

The concept of battle has to be one of the most fascinating of all human phenomena. Picture in your mind's eye, a landscape full of thousands of warriors resolutely marching off to battle – possibly never to return. In epic war movies like Braveheart, I am always struck by how the hero, flanked by a thousand men, marches bravely into battle with only the protection of a sword! Even more astonishing is the mindset that must prevail as they all proudly shout, "Today is a good day!"

What manner of courage (or madness) propels a person, against all odds, to hurl themselves at impossible goals – without batting an eyelid? Could this be a distant metaphor for what life sometimes requires? Going for broke?

What is it that inspires a person to throw all caution to the wind over a single cause? William Wallace of Scotland did this against the armies of England, as did Maximus against Rome, and Okonkwo against the offending invaders, and David against mighty Goliath of the Philistines. Perhaps, in explaining why he so frequently charged into battle with such fearlessness and ferocity, William Wallace said it best:

"Every man dies, but not every man truly lives!"

Apple CEO Steve Jobs is famous for saying, at a Stanford commencement speech, that every morning when he awakens, he checks to see if he is living in line with his purpose. Here's the story he told:

When I was 17, I read a quote that went something like: "If you live each day as if it was your last, someday you'll most certainly be right." It made an impression on me, and since then, for the past 33 years, I have looked in the mirror every morning and asked myself: "If today were the last day of my life, would I want to do what I am about to do today?" And whenever the answer has been "No" for too many days in a row, I know I need to change something.

Remembering that I'll be dead soon is the most important tool I've ever encountered to help me make the big choices in life. Because almost everything — all external expectations, all pride, all fear of embarrassment or failure - these things just fall away in the face of death, leaving only what is truly important. Remembering that you are going to die is the best way I know to avoid the trap of thinking you have something to lose. You are already naked. There is no reason not to follow your heart (Stanford News Service, 2005).

Joseph Campbell, one of the all-time gurus on the art of living, described the paradox of the hero's journey (Campbell, 1990). When you are willing to lose everything to follow your "bliss", you are entering into the hero's journey. When you find that where you have stumbled is where your treasures lie, you are on the hero's journey. When you fearlessly state your purpose, and it becomes the thing that you *must* manifest, you are on the hero's journey.

If you really want to find that which you seek, you are required to clearly determine your purpose upfront and then fearlessly go all the way toward achieving it. You cannot waver, and you must not bend to the pressures and distractions of things that are outside your purpose. If you cannot smile on your last day and say about your purpose, "it was worth it," then it's not worth another moment of your life's journey. Welcome to the story of you, where mediocre attempts are simply not good enough.

> It is an ideal, which I hope to live for and to achieve. But if needs be, it is an ideal for which I am prepared to die.
>
> – Nelson Mandela

The Parable Of The Bush Rat And The Lizard

Many years ago, before I came to the United States, I went to my grandfather's hut and asked him for advice. I asked him what I ought to do with myself when I get to America, which he liked to call 'the land of milk and honey'. This was his response:

"A bush rat should never fight in the rain with a lizard!"

What he was saying through that parable is that I needed to find out exactly what my purpose is, and then make sure to stick to whatever it is. The bush rat doesn't fare very well in the rain, so it would surely lose in a rain-fight with a lizard, which more than makes up for its smaller size because of its proclivity to thrive in wet environments.

In his own way, my grandfather was advising me to find my unique role in the world, and go 'be' my purpose. I wish I had taken his advice much earlier!

I believe strongly in the idea that every living thing has a unique purpose on our planet. Since we are interdependent, I also believe that there is a link between an individual's purpose and their ultimate success within the larger community. Without being able to prove this empirically, I believe that we are all part of a larger order – a structured, intelligent system – and the parts in that system all contribute to the good of the whole.

There is much social science research about how individual entities thrive when they are 'useful' to themselves and to the larger whole. In Charles Darwin's theory of natural selection, biological traits that are helpful for a species' reproduction become more popular and get passed on to future generations, while harmful traits become more rare. This process ensures that the species will survive and thrive. This is not too dissimilar to free market economics, in which businesses that supply what the market demands will thrive, and those that don't will eventually die off.

If you ever feel like you are just not doing what you're supposed to be doing, you might take my grandfather's advice and ask yourself: "am I a bush rat fighting in the lizard's rain?" If my grandfather's advice is too strange, use Steve Jobs' advice: *change* something.

> It is no fun to get to the mountaintop, only to discover it was the wrong one.
>
> - Pelè Raymond Ugboajah, PhD

Clarify And Write Down Your Purpose

In the early stages of my own story, I had always struggled with deciding clearly what my purpose was. I was the ultimate bush rat. In fact, for many years, lack of clarity was probably the one thing that held me back the most. I wasted so many years without a clear plan. For example, I actually went through nine years of architectural school education at the University level – *nine years* – only to discover later on that architecture simply wasn't my purpose!

I once used to wonder how much more I could have achieved with those same nine years if I had been directing my efforts at the current purpose of my life. What I've learned is that my struggles singled me out to be very interested in the topic of purpose, so it was all worth it in the end. It was my destiny to struggle through indecision so I could learn how to someday help others.

Today, my purpose is clear: to help *others* find their purpose.

> In the absence of clearly defined goals, we become strangely loyal to performing daily trivia until ultimately, we become enslaved by it.
>
> - Robert Heinlein

Having a clear, documented purpose, vision, or mission statement – whatever you choose to call it – is one of the best ways to ensure that you will reach your goals. A Dominican University of California study by Dr. Gail Matthews found that writing down one's intentions was a strong determinant of successful goal achievement (Matthews, 2008). In Dr. Matthews' study, a group of 149 participants recruited from various businesses and networking groups were asked to pursue certain goals, some by writing them down upfront, others by only thinking about them. Those who wrote down their goals achieved significantly more than those who didn't.

(Incidentally, this is *not* the celebrated Yale or Harvard study about writing down goals, which turns out to have been little more than an urban myth).

It is absolutely debilitating to be stuck – knowing you have passion, potential, and promise for something, but not know in which direction to put your efforts. After all my years of searching, I had to sit down one day, and once and for all, clarify and write down my purpose.

People are most productive and successful when they feel a strong, unshakable sense of purpose. However, it is one thing to write down a purpose, and another thing to write down the *wrong* purpose. How does one discover or decide on the *right* purpose for their lives?

The Purpose Wheel

The purpose of a game is to win. However, the purpose of the game of life is to help others win. In soccer, the purpose of the game is to score a goal in the opponent's goal post. In life, your purpose is to find congruence with the gifts, talents, and preferences you've been blessed with, so that you can put them to good use in the provision of value to yourself and others.

It is important to distinguish between dreams and purpose. Your dreams are a cherished ideal or situation that you might aspire to, but your purpose represents a much higher concept: the very *reason* for your existence. The former might be something you want, but the latter is something you were meant to do. You can have several dreams, but only one purpose. Indeed, when your dreams come true, they should all contribute to the overall purpose of your life – the reason you exist.

When you operate from your purpose, your bliss, whatever you truly desire – whatever you dream – you can certainly achieve. However, there is a caveat. The results you get will be dependent on many variables, some of which you can control, and others you can't. Your purpose can be found at the confluence of three variables from your already-lived story: (a) activities you are passionate about, (b) activities you have skills for, and (c) activities about which you have received positive feedback:

a) Passion

b) Skills

c) Feedback

Whatever your purpose may be, it should be something you are passionate about. Second, what you do with your life should leverage certain natural skills with which you've been endowed. And finally, you should have learned something in your past through feedback from others, (or the market), that can help you decide if what you dream about makes practical sense in the larger society.

If, for example you've received lots of personal satisfaction and positive external feedback regarding something you've done, then it might make sense to consider that as close to your purpose. If, however, you have continually learned that something you want to do is not good for you or others, then that will also help you in your decision process. Sometimes, you may be good at doing something, but feel no strong desire to do it. In such a case, it might be pointless to devote your life to it. In the end, you must consider several factors together before putting your final stake in the ground.

> "Don't ask what the world needs. Ask what makes you come alive, and go do it. Because what the world needs is people who have come alive"
>
> – Howard Thurman

How To Identify Your Purpose

Here's a process I developed for helping to discern one's unique purpose at the confluence of their passions, skills, and feedback. First, start by brainstorming all the different activities that you enjoy doing, and then rank each of them on a scale of 1-10 using the dimensions of passion, skill and feedback.

For example, when thinking about being an artist, ask yourself, "how passionate am I really about art, or is it just a means to another end for me?" Next, do I really have top-notch artistic skill? Can I develop it? Finally, ask yourself, what has the world told me about my art? Have I been complimented or paid handsomely for my art, or have I been consistently told *not* to quit my day job?

Here's a rough sample:

Activity you enjoy.	Passion Rank	Skill Rank	Feedback Rank	Total
Artist	3	8	7	18
Musician	8	7	8	23
Writer	7	7	7	21
Politics	1	0	1	2
Making Money	4	6	5	15
Speaker	8	9	10	27

Next, add up all the results in order to get a sense of which activities seem to receive the highest scores. After that, plot out each potential activity on the following 3-D matrix in terms of the dimensions of passion, skills, and feedback. The activity that has the highest scores for the combination of passion, skills and feedback will be somewhere in the middle and top-right section of the cube.

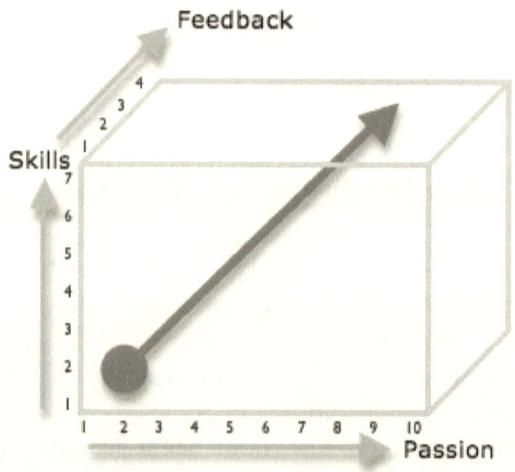

Your purpose should involve activities that have relatively high scores on all three dimensions. It is important to note that the 'highest' score from the first table exercise might not be the best choice, since you might rate certain things extremely high on one of the axes. The sweet spot is found in the third dimension – where all three dimensions are high – usually at the tip of the arrow in the upper-right quadrant, which recedes the furthest because of high positive feedback scores.

High passion and skill scores with low positive feedback could signify a purpose that is not useful to others. High skills and great feedback from the world is useless to you if you have no personal passion for what you do. Similarly, lots of great feedback from people about something you're passionate about, but for which you really don't possess sustainable skills could mean you're not getting truthful feedback.

What is Your Life's Purpose?

Your life has a unique purpose, whether you are aware of it or not. The purpose you are not aware of is the most dangerous because it is driving your actions from the shadows. It might be a purpose created and hidden within you from external inputs, such as societal or peer pressure. It could also be a faulty purpose that is driven by unexamined internal value systems. It is better to know what it is that is driving you, and even better to proactively decide what you *want* driving you.

> All men should strive to learn before they die, what they are running from, and to, and why.
>
> - James Thurber

Once you choose and commit to a purpose, you've taken the most important step in your life. Paulo Coelho, when asked what was the most difficult decision in his life, said that it was choosing finally to what he would commit his life. At around the age of forty, he abandoned all distractions and picked the most powerful and most meaningful purpose in his life: to be a writer. He committed to that single purpose, and put everything he had into it. No looking back.

That single decision led him to write *The Alchemist*, which is today ranked as one of the highest selling novels of all time.

One of my favorite tests for whether I am actually living my purpose is something attributed to Jim Collins, author of *Good to Great*. It is known as the 20:10 test:

> If you had $20 Million dollars in your pocket, and only 10 years to live, would you be doing what you are doing today?

If your answer is 'yes' – congratulations! You are already living within your purpose. This exercise helps to eliminate the distraction of money and material things from your considerations of purpose. It helps you focus less on gaining the world, and more on securing what's most meaningful to your soul.

Story Assessment #1: Purpose

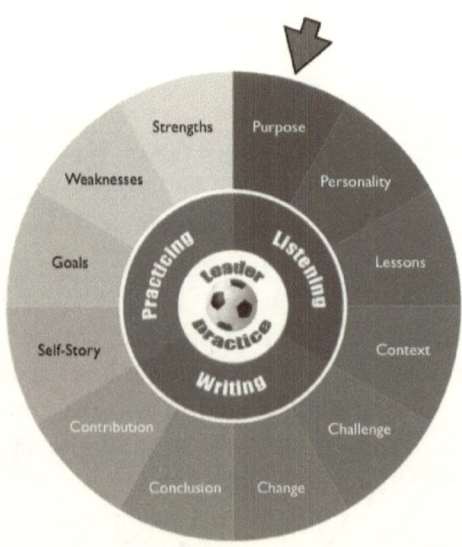

What activities are you most passionate about?

_____

_____

_____

_____

_____

What skills that are you most proud of, which give you the most personal satisfaction?

_____

_____

_____

_____

_____

Which of your skills or activities have had the most positive feedback from others?

_____

_____

_____

_____

Pelè Raymond Ugboajah, PhD

On a scale of 1 to 10, rate the activities you enjoy doing against your level of passion for them, your level of skill, and the level of feedback you've received about them.

Activity you enjoy.	Passion Rank	Skill Rank	Feedback Rank	Total

Using a blank sheet of paper, draw a 3D box similar to the one on page 76. Which of your highlighted activities has the highest overall position in that 3D matrix view of passion, skills, and feedback?

_____

If you were given $20 Million dollars and 10 years to live, write down what you would do with the money and the time.

_____

_____

_____

Going forward, the following activities should be part of my life's purpose.

_____

_____

_____

In once sentence, *this* is my life's purpose.

Is your purpose above congruent with what you are doing today?

At a certain, critical decision point in your life, you will be faced with a decision about your purpose. If you choose to heed the call, you must be prepared and willing to sacrifice everything for it. The irony of living is that when we are willing to lose it all, we *gain* everything.

You cannot afford to be afraid to fail, for when you remove all opportunities for failure, you simultaneously remove all opportunities for success. Choose your purpose carefully, then commit yourself, square your shoulders and stand firm.

If you will *be* your purpose, your purpose will come to be!

7.

Personality

Man's main task in life is to give birth to himself, to become what he potentially is. The most important product of his effort is his own personality.
– ERICH FROMM

There was once an old bar, deeply set in an old farm town – the kind of town where everyone knew everyone's name. You grew up here and still carry many fond memories, but you've been gone for almost ten years now. Today you're back for a school reunion, and you thought you'd stop over at the old bar. You know most people in this town, but from the corner of your eye, you catch a glimpse of someone you've never seen before – an old man sitting alone in the corner – dirty, disheveled, and worn. You notice that the man is engaged in a deep, personal consultation with a bottle of cheap whiskey.

He looks like an irresponsible beggar, and everyone seems to avoid him like the plague.

You walk up to Jim, the bartender, and ask about the old man. Jim frowns, and quietly asks you to sit down, grab a drink, so he can explain. It turns out that there is much more here than meets-the-eye. According to Jim, the old man was once the owner of the bar, and was also the richest man in town. That was until his only son left for the Iraq war and never returned, his wife of 30 years died suddenly, and all of his investments collapsed along with the nation's last financial crisis. The old man now comes into the bar each day, at the same time, and sits alone. He bothers no one, and no one bothers him.

Now, looking at him again, you understand! No longer do you see the irresponsible beggar everyone is avoiding. Instead you see someone who has experienced extremely difficult times – someone people are respectfully leaving alone. Listening to his story made all the difference in the world.

> Don't judge a book by its cover.
> To fully understand your personality, you need the whole story.

In my early days as a leadership development coach, I frequently helped large organizations select and determine the 'fit' of their in-coming leaders. We would conduct detailed psychological assessments to determine personality, values, motivations, and potential leadership and behavioral derailers. After the assessments, we would involve the executives in role-plays to learn how they might respond to leadership challenges in real-time. From all of this data, we would compare our results against the desired leadership competencies of the organization and provide a detailed, qualitative report on the leader's personality and potential.

But we missed the most important detail of all.

We never delved deeply into the leader's *story*. How did she get here? What narrative events can help explain the triggers for this or that behavior? What experiences have led her to become the type of personality she is today?

All of these kinds of questions go one crucial level deeper into the qualitative assessment process, where a person's actual life narrative becomes part of the assessment resource. If organizations took the time to conduct more detailed narrative assessments, they would have much less turnover and leadership failure.

> Story-Listening is a qualitative assessment process that helps us make sense of the past, understand the present, and position ourselves for a better future.

Story: The Assessment Beyond Psychology

Your personality is not only what you or others see on the surface. Rather, you behave as you do today because of both innate behavioral preferences, and learned behaviors acquired from the life *story* you've lived. Your personality is therefore best understood as a *combination* of what you and others know about your behavior, with what your life and business stories – your narrative – has shown you to be. Story-Listening therefore involves the combined use of standard psychological assessment tools with a qualitative, narrative inquiry into a subject's already-lived life.

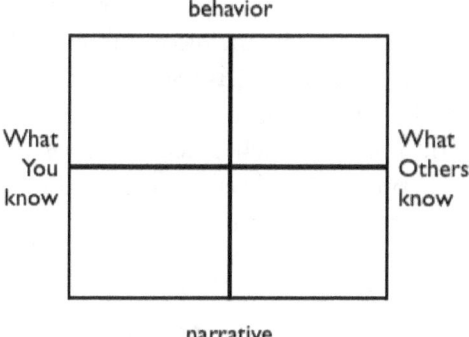

The following groups of information come together to deliver a more complete qualitative assessment of your personality:

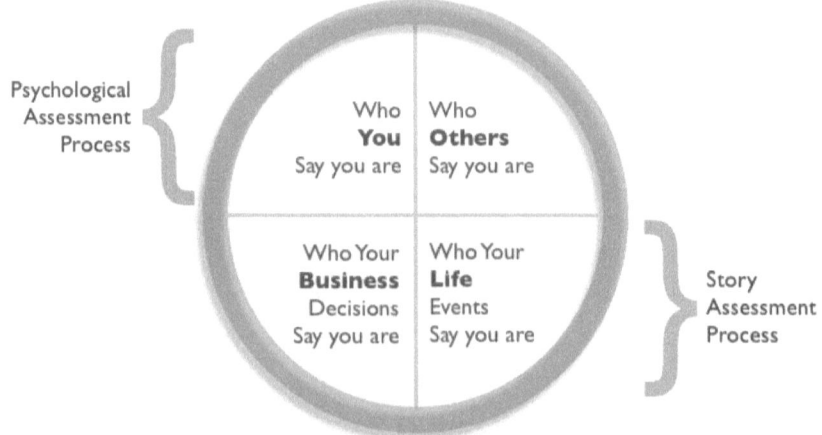

1. What you know about your behavior
2. What others know about your behavior
3. What specific narratives reveal about you
4. What others see in those specific narratives

Most leadership development methods use a 'black-box' psychological assessment approach – featuring hidden discovery formulas and seemingly unrelated multiple-choice questions – to supply only a current snapshot of a person's *behavior*. (What you know about your behavior). The inclusion of 360° information (what others know about your behavior) is useful, but still only provides a snapshot, and not the whole story.

The output of this approach is certainly predictive of future performance, but it provides little or no practical guidance regarding one's personal *narrative*. (What you and others know about specific events in your life and business story). The Story-Listening approach is a more complete predictor of where a person's unconscious internal forces may be driving them, because it combines their current psychological information with key catalytic life events that may be driving certain aspects of their behavior.

Organizations and employees alike should learn more about an individual's complete story, because therein lies their potential for greatness, not to mention the hidden forces that will either keep them productive, or eventually send them out the door.

Story Assessment #2: Personality

How would you describe your behavior and personality? If you've taken psychological assessments in the past, include what you've learned about your personality here:

_____

_____

_____

_____

Write down the three best aspects of your personality.

_____

_____

_____

How would those who know you or work closest with you describe
your behavior? Ask three people to tell you three things they think
are best about your personality. Write them down.

_____

_____

_____

_____

Ask three people to tell you three things you should change in your
interactions with people in life or at work. Write them down.

_____

_____

_____

_____

_____

_____

Think of some defining, catalytic events that have happened in your personal and professional life. How did you respond to them? What do these experiences exemplify about your personality?

_____

_____

_____

_____

_____

Ask three people to recall some experiences they've shared with you that could be used to exemplify certain aspects of your personality. Write them down.

_____

_____

_____

_____

_____

Within your story lies a wealth of qualitative narrative information, which can enrich and compliment traditional psychological assessments. Story-Listening helps you to combine these two forms of inquiry into a richer, mixed-methods 'story assessment', which is useful for explaining how you got to where you are today, and also for revealing what you'll need in order to create lasting success for tomorrow.

8.

Lessons

Life is a succession of lessons, which must be lived to be understood.
– HELEN KELLER

The summer I left my last corporate job, I was able to go on vacation for a few weeks. I had hit a wall, a mid-life crisis of sorts, and simply wasn't sure what to do with the rest of my life and career. I decided to take a short trip to Florida. While I was there, I ran into a wonderful little book: *If Life Is A Game, These Are The Rules*, by Dr. Cherie Carter-Scott. A central premise of the book was a simple idea: we live in order to learn; and that life is the ultimate teacher, providing us with unique lessons that we will either choose to learn from or ignore as time goes by. If we learn our lessons, we move on to higher levels of learning, but if we ignore them, life continues to present them to us over and over and over, until we finally learn what they are trying to teach us (Carter-Scott, 1998).

This simple idea got me thinking. It occurred to me that life must teach us these unique lessons for a reason, so that we can grow closer to our purpose, and become the very best that we can be. I started to see my life's lessons as the beginning template for creating a more purposeful 'story of me'.

> **Life will present lessons – sometimes disguised - to illuminate your purpose. It is up to you to recognize them.**

This led me into a deep exploration and re-assessment of myself. I sought to understand how I had ended up doing the things I had done, and why I chose the specific careers I did. Halfway through this exercise, it realized that my research was not dissimilar from what a doctor might do with a new client – 'diagnosing' a person's story in order to accurately prescribe something for the future.

However, there was a key difference between what I was doing, and what most psychological instruments measure. I was going deeper than personality or trait measurements. Instead of exclusively examining current, observable behavioral patterns, I was also evaluating historical *life events* and *business decisions*.

Together, these elements provided a broader view of my life and business than the static snapshot of most standard psychological assessments. I found myself answering questions like, "why did you join *that* company?" or "what did you learn when you quit *that* job?" I was essentially building a case history of all the patterns, transitions, decisions, and events in my life that would help me make an informed diagnosis of who I really am, and what I really ought to do with my life going forward.

I was looking for strengths as much as weaknesses. Far too much of modern psychology looks to the past to discover what went *wrong*, yet it is sometimes what went *right* that is most useful in helping people create the best future story for their lives. In this case, one has to look for the best information from both worlds.

For example, following is a chart outlining the kinds of discovery one can do to isolate the lessons that life has been trying to teach you through your career. On the left is the year and the vocation or activity that you were involved in at the time. To the right are three questions for each period in your life: (a) why you started the job or activity, (b) why the activity ended, and (c) what lesson(s) you learned about yourself as a result.

Year	Vocation	Why did I start?	Why did it end?	Lesson(s) Learned?
1987	School			
1992	First Job			
Etc.	Etc.			

At each step, you have to ask yourself, "Why did I get involved in this?" Following that, you should ask yourself "why did it end?" And to round out each section, you should write down (honestly) what *learning* you gained about yourself from that event.

The purpose of this exercise is to arm you visually with all the lessons you have (or should have) learned throughout your already-lived life story. This kind of assessment will not only give you a sense of who you are, it will show who you aren't as well. You will learn that there are certain things you shouldn't be doing because you'll find that life has already taught you lessons in that area, sometimes multiple times.

Now, armed with these lessons, you'll have a clearer sense of what you should uniquely do to be in line with your purpose and personality as you seek to design your future success.

After listening to my story, here are some of the specific lessons I uncovered:

1. My life's purpose and goal is to help others find their purpose as I've found mine. I want to help change lives.

2. I care most about using my creative abilities of music, motivation, and mentorship, to bring enlightenment and development to others. I am incomplete when some of my creative talents, (such as music), are ignored in the pursuit of my purpose.

3. Life taught me that within corporate walls, I am at best an 'intrapreneur'. As a result of my passion for innovation and driving change, I am more of an entrepreneur than an employee. I therefore needed to cast away the fear, and jump

toward my entrepreneurial destiny – regardless of financial returns.

4.   I found that my skills – music, motivation, and mentorship – were congruent with my purpose. I was ready to go.

My Important Career Lesson

In 1996 I wrote and produced six songs for Alexander O'Neal on EMI records, a major label record company. At the time, I was a budding entrepreneur and songwriter, committed to innovation and business independence. To give you a sense of what this accomplishment in the music industry meant to me, this is an artist who was discovered by Prince, had scored numerous top-charting R&B hits such as *Fake* and *Criticize*, and had already sold millions of records during his career. The team of Jimmy Jam and Terry Lewis, who were two of the greatest R&B/POP songwriter/producers of all time, had been the previous producers on most of his records. In many ways, Alexander O'Neal was an R&B legend, and there I was, writing and producing his songs!

This was my first major label deal and I was thrilled! It also turned out to be my last. EMI Records dropped Alexander O'Neal very shortly after our album was released. As a result, our record, *Lovers Again*, did not receive as much funding or marketing support as might be expected of a sustained major label effort. Nonetheless, my six songs on the album still spawned a couple of hits, including *Let's Get Together*, which got to #58 on America's Billboard chart. Today, the album is still in moderate rotation as an 'oldie but goodie' in parts of Europe.

I left the music industry shortly after this album was released, and I learned a very important lesson. Since 1996, I have received quarterly royalty income from those six songs. No other job I had ever left has continued to pay me residual income! After my entrepreneurial adventure in the music industry, I joined the corporate world and worked in various middle management leadership positions. However, in 2002, as a result of a merger, and I was laid off – with absolutely *nothing* to show for my years of hard work, six-figure salary, and fancy corner office. It was over, just like that!

This episode taught me the difference – and my preference – between two business models: employment versus entrepreneurship. I came away realizing that I prefer to work either as an entrepreneur in my own business, or as an employee in a business environment that encourages and appreciates entrepreneurship. I also learned that I prefer to create works that will continue to produce recurring, residual income – long after the work has been done.

I do not know how else these lessons could have been burned so indelibly in my consciousness, but I am very thankful I learned them. In many ways, you have to experience some things to really learn the lessons attached to them. These unique lessons have now become an integral part of my self-story. They are now part of the fabric of who I am.

After I got laid off in 2002, I tried to rejoin the work force, but never bothered to include this music industry story as part of my resume. Like most job seekers, I was in a 'selling' mode, so I included only what was most positive and pertinent to the job I was seeking. As a result, I left out some of the most important lessons I had learned because (a) they would not fit within a few pages of a resume, (b) I feared that saying I was more passionate about entrepreneurship might disqualify me, and (c) I thought it probably wasn't relevant to the job I was seeking anyway. So, like most people, I left out critical information that might have been very useful in the interview process. Also, no one interviewing me asked any probing *positive* questions about my story, and therefore never learned just how important things like innovation, ownership, and residual income models were to me. Yet, these were the kinds of things that I personally could not live without in a business situation.

What I have since learned is that our leadership selection and development systems leave out a lot of truth if we assess and interview people without really listening *deeply* to their stories. Employers may find someone who will do a decent job in the short term, but that person will rarely be truly satisfied until whatever lessons they've learned in life are addressed in their work. To truly know a person, you have to listen to their self-story, the ultimate collection of their life-lessons.

No wonder the world of business ends up with the following statistics: only 20% of employees are 'passionate' about their jobs (PR Newswire, 2008); 50 % of highly paid executives are dissatisfied with their jobs (ExecuNet, 2007); 80% of HR executives believe that their companies don't do a good job of developing leaders (HR Policy Association, 2008). Organizations are forfeiting a lot of important, qualitative leadership assessment information when they rely exclusively on resumes and psychological surveys. How can you really hire or develop a leader whose story you simply don't know?

Story Assessment #3: Lessons

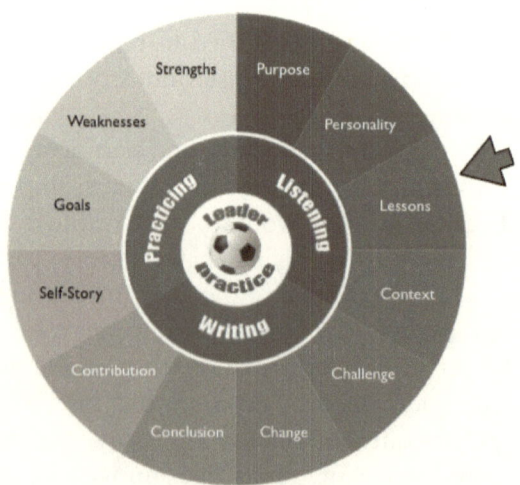

Think back to all the different jobs or business ventures you've ever had. In the following table, write each one down, and write down why you started it, why you left it, and what unique lesson(s) you learned from each experience:

Year	Vocation	Why did you start?	Why did it end?	Lesson(s) Learned?

What do you care most about? What aspect of all the lessons you've learned are deal-breakers for you in future decisions? What must you have in any business venture you are involved in?

_____

_____

_____

_____

What have you discovered yourself to be? Are you a good team player? Employee? Entrepreneur? Investor? Are you an innovator or an adapter? Write down what you've learned about your unique work style and preferences:

_____

_____

_____

_____

_____

What have you learned about your life outside of work?

_____

_____

_____

What have you learned about your relationships with people?

This process of personal discovery helped me go forth with strong, personal conviction. I was ready to march into battle! I felt very comfortable that I could write and tell this self-story convincingly to my unconscious mind.

Psychological tests that tell you whether or not you're extroverted are fine, but they only touch at the surface of your *personality*. Without a full review and documentation of your life's *purpose*, as well as the many wonderful *lessons* in your already-lived story, you will never know what might be working for or against you in your life and work. You are more than a psychological assessment. Take some time away from your daily grind, and go listen to the story of you.

STORY-WRITING

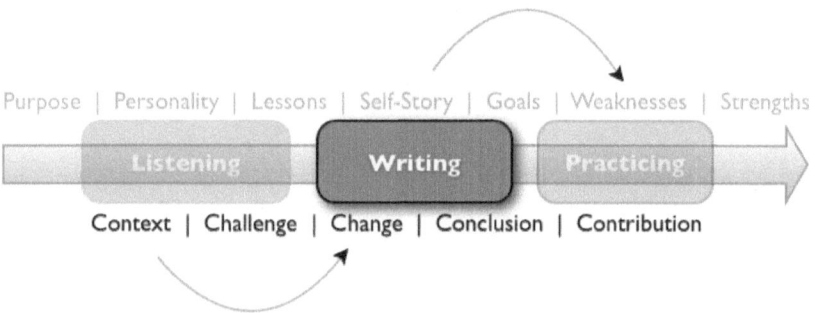

Heretofore, we've been discussing the process and principles involved in Story-listening. Now, in the following section, we'll switch gears to **Story-writing**, which is the process of creating your future story design. We will use the five 'acts' of your story – a standard narrative framework that will help you design your own success story:

1. Context – how you got here.

2. Challenge – your urgency for change.

3. Change – what action you, the hero, will take.

4. Conclusion – what your results will be.

5. Contribution – why it'll be all worth doing.

By the end of this section, you'll be ready to move to the next skill – Story-practicing – where you will turn the ideas and goals you've written into actions that will lead you into your future success story.

9.

Context

Priority is a function of context.
– STEPHEN R. COVEY

For most of us, life shows up out of the blue like a drama already half-told. We find ourselves in the middle of an elaborate, detailed set of circumstances, but we're not always aware of the larger context. We recognize stories all around us: on the news, in the movie theaters, and in books – but we almost never realize that the most important story we can influence, is our own.

We don't always have, in present focus, all the complexities and intricacies of who we are and how we got here, and to make matters worse, there is not much energy left for deep reflection after a hard day's work. Things are moving way too fast! If we could only just stop and listen, we'd be able to develop a much better sense of who we've been, who we are, and who we want to be going forward.

Every good story starts with a clear context: a sense of *where you are and how you got here*. On the next page is a Story-Writing framework for designing your self-story, starting with the first thing first: your context.

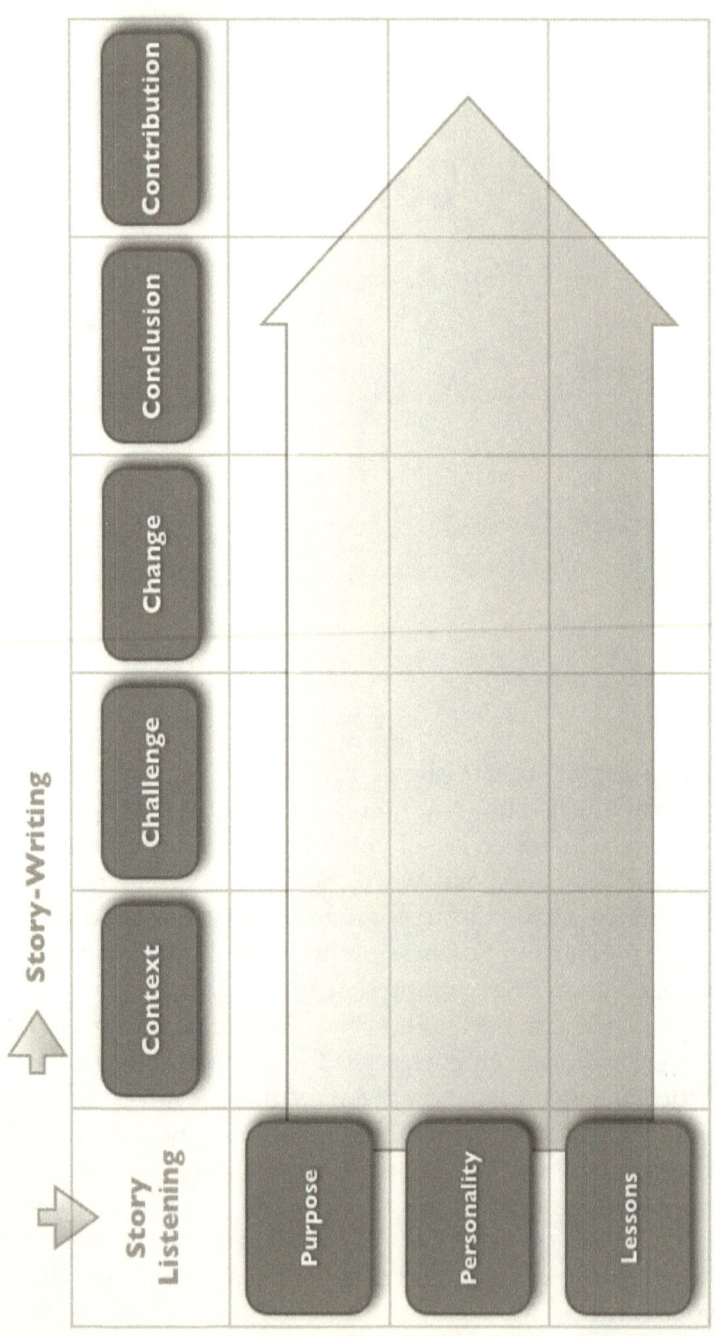

The Story-Writing framework consists of two axes. On the y-axis will be the results of your Story-Listening exploration into your purpose, personality and lessons, while on the x-axis you'll document the five Cs of your story, (context, challenge, change, conclusion, and contribution). In the Story-Writing phase, your task is to use the five Cs as a framework to storyboard what you desire as future life or work outcomes, given what you now know about yourself. This means that you'll need to write down how each of these three Story-Listening dimensions, (purpose, personality, and lessons) will be impacted as you move through the five Cs of your story.

Let's take a look at how to fill out the context section of your story:

Context

This is where you will summarize all that you've learned about yourself so far from Story-Listening to your three dimensions of purpose, personality, and lessons. If you've done all the exercises so far, here's what you should know about yourself:

1. You are now very clear about what your unique life **purpose** is, and you have it written down. You reviewed your passion, skills, and feedback, and identified your purpose at the confluence of those three dimensions.

2. You are clear on your **personality**, with special emphasis on your strengths and weaknesses. In terms of behavior, you should now have a list of what to do more of, and what to avoid.

3. You are now clear on what **lessons** life has uniquely been trying to teach you, and you are committed to not re-learning those particular lessons.

The cumulative output of these dimensions is the content you will use to pen your compelling and self-influential self-story. Following is an example of a self-story structure in the context section of the story of you:

Story Assessment #4: Context

The context of your story is 'how you got here' — a summary of the things you've learned by exploring the dimensions of your purpose, personality, and lessons-learned. Write them down.

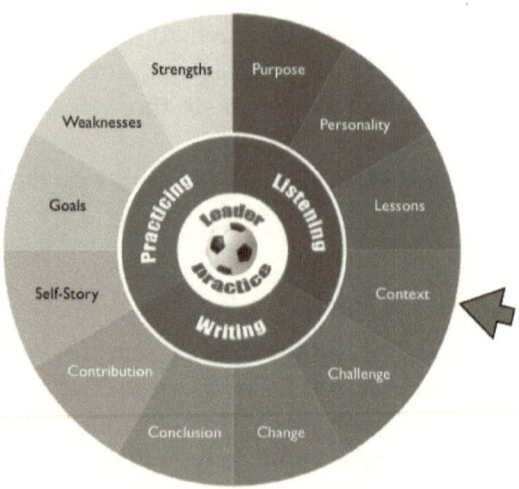

Based on reviewing your passion, skills and feedback, the purpose of your life and work is:

_____

_____

_____

_____

_____

Your personality consists of the following strengths and weaknesses, which you will maximize and minimize respectively:

Strengths:

_____

_____

_____

_____

_____

Weaknesses:

_____

_____

_____

_____

_____

The lessons you have learned about yourself through your past life and business decisions are:

_____

_____

_____

_____

_____

How To Write The Other Four Acts Of Your Story

After writing the context section, you will be armed with enough information to begin moving forward into the next four sections of the story of you. Here's a preview of the kind of content you will want to capture in the following four acts of your story.

Challenge

In the next section, (challenge), you will write out what is going on right now in your life. Here, you will describe your level of *urgency* for taking action. What is your current challenge? How is it affecting your life or work purpose? Is it a distraction, or is what is happening in your life congruent with your purpose? How are your current challenges affecting your personality and vice-versa? How are you responding to things as they are happening? Finally, you should indicate what lessons you're currently learning. Are you on a path to re-learn any lessons you should have already learned?

Change

In the change section, you will start to indicate what you, the hero, must do differently in order to achieve different or better results. What are your desired outcomes? Paying close attention to your purpose, personality and life lessons, how will you address the current challenges? Who else will be affected by your changes? What are your planned changes with respect to family, friends, or colleagues? How will you incorporate what you've learned about your strengths? How will you be careful to minimize your weaknesses so that they don't become personal or leadership derailers along the way?

Conclusion

In the conclusion section, you will start with the end in mind, and write out a statement of what the future will look like when your work is done. Knowing what you are today in terms of purpose, personality and life lessons, who will you have become at the end of your story? What will have happened to the people in your life?

What effect on society will your efforts have produced? This is where you write down the story that ninety-five year-old you will be able to recall and tell to others about your life.

Contribution

Finally, in the last section, (contribution), you will write out what you will be leaving behind. What will have been the single contribution that you would have brought to your family, your work, your society, or mankind as a whole? What would they all say that you have *given* to the world?

10.

Challenge

Without a sense of urgency, desire loses its value.
– JIM ROHN

I'll never forget the morning of June 22ⁿᵈ, 2002. I had just gotten a cup of hot office coffee, and had settled down to review my emails in my corner office at the top of the France Towers in Edina, Minnesota. I had arrived at what most people would call the 'American Dream'. At the time, I was a highly paid Director of Marketing for a $20 Billion (US) dollar organization. I had reached the top of the mountain and everything was going great except for one thing: it was the wrong mountain!

I was really struggling with the whole idea of playing company politics. Somebody forgot to pass me the memo about political savvy being the key requirement for both survival and success in the corporate game.

I had never been any good at office politics, because I had this unfortunate habit of wanting to speak my mind in meetings. At the time, I felt strongly that advancing in the corporate world was about getting results. Turns out I was wrong – at least in *that* company. I was lousy at the art of sucking up to my superiors. I thought I was doing a great job, and the results could show that easily. But I hadn't worked hard enough to be *loved* by the powers that be.

That morning, the phone rang, and my boss was on the other end of it. In a very unemotional, detached voice, he said: "In yesterday's merger meeting we decided to downsize. Unfortunately, today will be your last day at $20 Billion Dollar Organization!"

(Okay – maybe he didn't say it quite like that!)

In any case, that was that. My corporate ladder ran out of rungs. No warning. No potential for negotiation. It was over, just like that.

My daughter was barely a year old at the time, and things were not going well on the home front either. Shortly after getting fired from my day job, my spouse filed for divorce, No warning. No potential for negotiation. It was over just like that.

In a few short months I had lost my job and my wife, and could only see my daughter every other weekend by driving up to the curb of my former home.

I just couldn't see how life was fair.

So, I packed all my belongings, got into my truck, and began driving south – determined to go wherever and however far my gasoline tank would take me. Along the way, I fell very ill, and ended up in a Florida hospital. My diagnosis? High blood pressure! I thought I was going to die, and I am not ashamed to admit that I was fine with that. I just didn't care that much about living anymore.

But somehow I didn't give up.

I was in the middle of some serious life challenges, but something in my programming helped me get up, as it has, time and time again. Instead of crumbling and withering away, I started returning to my roots, reinventing myself, and rediscovering my passion. This time, I was focused on pursuing my destiny, instead of corporate titles and paychecks. I was determined to make something of myself – and never be fired again.

I am still amazed at how things turned around for me after I made that commitment. I changed my mind about Florida, and returned to Minnesota to be closer to my daughter. Initially, friends and family loaned me money, and I eventually returned to school to complete my PhD instead of getting another corporate position.

During that time, I went back to music, my original passion, and began writing and singing songs anywhere I could. I also joined

Toastmasters, and eventually won the 2006 International Public Speaking Competition for District 6. Along the way, I met Les Brown, one of the world's most renowned motivational speakers, and he was so impressed with me that he invited me to attend his $10,000 workshop in Florida – completely free. Later on, he asked me to work for him as his Vice President of Marketing. Over time, I wrote my first two books and eventually met the love of my life, to whom I am now married.

I never gave up! I didn't let my challenges define me. Instead, I used them to create the sense of urgency I needed for taking action. I believed again. Has this ever happened to you?

> Long ago, I believed
> I could fly, and reach the sky
> Over time, reality
> Broke my faith, and brought me rain
>
> After the storm was over
> And all I had was dreams
> All of a sudden I was free
> Because I believed
> Nothing is impossible ... if you believe
>
> Have you ever wished that you could reach and touch the sky?
> Have you ever wondered if it's possible to fly?
> Have you ever had a dream that suddenly came true?
> This is my story, and it can happen to you ...If You Believe.
>
> © Pele Raymond Ugboajah, PhD
> (You can download this song from www.LeaderPractice.com)

Everyone will at some point have a challenge, just like I did. Once upon a time, things were one way, and now, things are another way. In most stories, something goes wrong in the challenge phase –

sometimes, terribly wrong, and things fall apart. In the challenge phase, there is always a mystery to solve, a goal to pursue.

But every story's challenge has a level of difficulty that is in the eyes of each beholder. You, the hero, are the only one who can decide if what you have in front of you is a difficulty or an opportunity. You alone control what role you choose to play as you address your challenges.

> "A pessimist sees the difficulty in every opportunity, but an optimist sees the opportunity in every difficulty."
>
> - Winston Churchill

The key to creating the future you desire is to thoroughly understand your past context, your current challenges, and clarify what role you will choose to play in your evolving story going forward. This combination of knowing your context and current challenges will position you to become a more proactive hero in your story.

As the hero of your story, you will need to:

1. Uncover the various opportunities inherent in your current challenges.

2. Leverage your current difficulties to create a sense of urgency for action.

3. Decide to proactively shape your future.

But first, you must begin to see your challenges, however difficult, from an optimistic point of view. Every cloud has a silver lining, but it's not always obvious. You must look for it!

Fully Understand, Before You Propose

You may have heard the saying: *it's hard to see the picture when you're in the frame.* Sometimes you have to step outside of the frame you're in to fully see the picture. Consider this ancient parable about an elephant and six blind men:

Once there were six blind scholars who guarded a village of blind people, and they were presented with an animal they had never known before. It was an elephant, and the villagers wanted a full description of the creature before allowing it into their village. So, each blind man went up to the elephant and gave a description.

The first blind man held on to the Elephant's tusk and declared: "an elephant is like a spear, very sharp and pointy!" The next blind man approached the elephant on its side, and said: "No, you're wrong, an elephant is like a wall, solid and dull!" The third blind man stumbled over to the elephant's tail, and holding it, announced: "you're both wrong; an elephant is like a rope, thin and tough!" Next, the fourth blind man held on to the elephant's trunk, and laughing, shouted: "You're all wrong! An elephant is like a snake, wriggly and soft!" Next,

the fifth blind man held onto the ear and declared: "Alas, an elephant is more like a fan!" Finally, the sixth blind man rubbed up against the elephant's knee and proclaimed: You are all very wrong. An elephant is like an old tree trunk, rough and sturdy!"

The men argued long and loud, until a stranger (who could see) came along, and pointed to the elephant saying: "Individually, you're all wrong, but together you're actually right!" The point of the parable is this: you can't fully describe the whole until you position yourself so you can see the total of all the parts.

The *challenge* phase of your story is happening right now – *today* – and it is up to you to identify and accurately describe your current life and business situation in full. Only through a complete and accurate definition of your problem can you proceed toward a solution. Most of us don't take the time and energy to really think through our current challenges. Instead, we live by default, reacting to things as they happen, and we make declarative statements such as "life is hard!"

If you've ever thought that life is hard, my question to you would be this: "Is it really? Or are you only seeing one part of the elephant?"

How To Find The Good In Your Challenges

Like moths to a flame, we are a problem-seeking species. Our minds are wired to see problems everywhere, and we are quick to identify the negative aspects of most situations. My father, referring to politics, used to say: "The biggest problem here is problem-definition!" He was right, and I think the same generally goes for our lives. However, I would add that even as we try to accurately define our problems, we must do more to resist our natural bias to see only the negative side of whatever life presents us.

Sometimes the most difficult challenges in life are actually the greatest opportunities we've ever had for reaching our goals. But we're frequently unable to see clearly in the moment, and we casually relegate things to the "problem" column, when in fact, they could be opportunities in disguise.

Even our everyday language is geared toward seeing the worst in situations. Next time you meet someone, ask him or her "how are you?" For many, the answer will be "Not bad!" Whatever happened to "Very good?" No wonder we start from the worst assumptions! The negative viewpoint is hard-wired into our daily communication and thinking patterns!

The secret to using the context and challenge phases of your story to create a future of success is to learn how to proactively and habitually view your challenges as opportunities. Here's an exercise that can help you start converting challenges into opportunities. Whenever you are being challenged write out the following:

Challenge	Cons	Pros	Conversion
I lost my job	I'm broke.	I can return to school and get my degree	I'll learn my lessons, get better prepared, and take my time to look for a better job.
Etc. etc.			
Etc. etc.			

The act of writing these down does not by itself solve your challenges for you. It just helps you start thinking in more than one singular, negative way. Instead of having your thoughts focused on only what's wrong, you'll develop the habit of always looking for what's potentially right about each situation.

An ancient Chinese parable also makes this point very clear. Once there was an old man who lost his horse. His neighbors felt sorry for him, but he said: "who knows? This could be a blessing." A few months later, the horse returned, and brought back another beautiful horse. His neighbors came over to congratulate him, but he dispassionately said: "who knows? This could be a disaster." As if by cue, his son took to riding the new horse, and one day fell down and broke his legs. Again the neighbors came to comfort the old man, but he said: "who knows? This could be a blessing." Sure enough, a few months later, a war broke out and all the young men were drafted into the war effort except his young son. Nine out of ten of those who left for the war were killed. The old man's son, being crippled from falling off the horse, was spared.

Remember Mandela's twenty-seven long years in prison, or the assassination of Martin Luther King, or the crucifixion of Jesus? Sometimes the worst tragedy is the greatest gift our purpose has ever been given. It all depends on your perspective – whether you use a story-point-of-view or not – as you observe your situation.

Mandela's years in prison led to the destruction of Apartheid, a feat no single man could have otherwise achieved. The martyrdom of Martin Luther King created an atmosphere in America that was finally empathetic to the dreams of the civil rights movement. And for Christians, the crucifixion of Jesus resulted in nothing less than the salvation of all mankind. A short-term point of view would have relegated all of those events to hopeless tragedies. However, a story point of view, which is much more long-term, would have seen the potential for great positive impacts down the road. It all depends on your perspective.

Life Is H.A.R.D.

It is from a challenge in a story that the hero is inspired to emerge and chase after the dragon, rescue the princess, and save the day. Your challenge reveals the urgency you need for your vision, and gives you fuel for the tasks ahead. It is up to you to examine your circumstances and reveal the opportunities within them. Here's a saying of mine, which sums up my view on hardship:

> **Life is not hard;**
> **Life is H.A.R.D. – How Adversity Reveals Destiny!**

One of my favorite motivational speakers, Willie Jolley, has a saying he has made famous: "a setback is a setup for a comeback!" I love that saying, because it really sits at the heart of how success can be created by people who find themselves in difficult situations.

Challenge and opportunity are intertwined, and they always go hand in hand. The hero in every great story must find a way to turn challenges into opportunities and create a sense of urgency for future success. Life is full of challenges, but it is through these challenges that our destinies are revealed.

Story Assessment #5: Challenge

What challenges do you currently face? What new (or old) lessons do you need to learn from them? What lessons might you be ignoring or resisting? What are your strengths, weaknesses, opportunities and threats? Write them all down!

Using the Story-Writing framework, write down your current challenges with respect to your purpose, personality, and lessons learned. Write down what opportunities are inherent in the current challenges you're facing. Write down how you intend to take advantage of those challenges, and turn adversity into destiny.

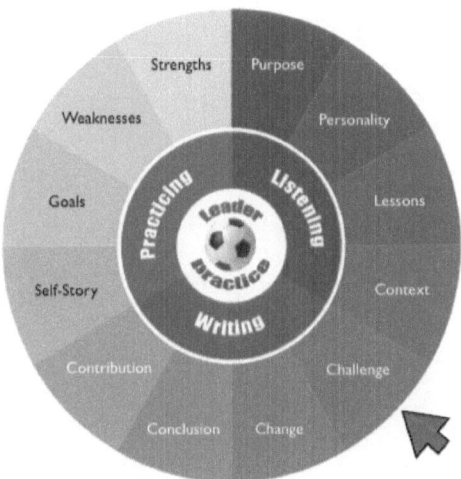

On the following page, write down the current challenges in your life, each followed by the pros, the cons, and the opportunity inherent in each difficulty:

Challenge	Cons	Pros	Conversion

How is your life's purpose affected by these challenges?

_____

_____

_____

_____

How will you maximize the strengths and minimize the weaknesses in your personality as you address these challenges?

_____

_____

_____

_____

_____

What is your level of urgency? How much do you *want* change? Are you inspired and motivated to turn these challenges into advantages in the service of your purpose? Why or why not?

_____

_____

_____

_____

It will be up to you to either grow from today's challenge or let it pile up in the category of lessons not learned. The output of Story-Listening is that you will gain a better sense of context, and meaning. You now know a lot more about how you got 'here' from 'there'. Now is the time to align what you've learned about yourself to a sense of urgency for the change that lies ahead.

11.

Change

The best way to predict your future is to create it!
– ABRAHAM LINCOLN

The change phase is where you, the hero, must take action! Great stories do a great job of showcasing change – that critical moment when the hero decides to follow his or her purpose. Usually, there is an epiphany, a change in priorities, and the hero will begin the journey from difficulty to opportunity, or from adversity to destiny.

In *The Lord of the Rings*, Frodo finds himself the unwitting protector of a very dangerous and powerful ring. He submits to the situation, and his destiny becomes forever intertwined with the ring. In *The Gladiator*, Maximus at first cannot believe how Commodus betrayed him and murdered his entire family, but he soldiers on, and his life's new quest leads him to become the greatest gladiator legend in ancient Rome. In *The Alchemist*, Santiago the shepherd boy reaches a point where he knows he must begin the journey to Egypt. He knows his destiny lies there, and despite the danger, he joins the desert caravan.

They all took action.

You know you are in the change phase when you have a critical decision that you must make, which could cost you everything. There is no plan 'B'. You're going for broke. You are ready for the change phase when you accept that you have no choice but to comply with your destiny.

> Nobody can go back and start a new beginning. But anyone can start today and make a new ending.
>
> – Maria Robinson

There comes a time in every story when the hero will decide to proactively write their own unique story, and start to see it through. I'll never forget the day it dawned on me that the changes I had started living out in my own story were finally producing results. I was finally living my purpose – free to pursue my own unique concept of success.

I was speaking to a crowd of hundreds of people at the Regional level of the Toastmasters International Speaking competition. Already the District champion, I was just one step away from the final International competition. I had also just finished composing one of my motivational songs – "If You Believe" – and had distributed it to several people along with a chapter from a book I was planning at the time. As I looked out at the audience, I realized I was home. In their eyes was an eagerness to learn what I was about to teach, and in my heart was the message that God had planned for them to hear that evening. The speech went great, and I could see several tear-filled eyes staring at me as they applauded at the end.

Later on, outside the meeting room, one of the audience members came up to me and said: "That was the best, most life-changing speech I have ever heard. Thank you." Later on, another person, a friend who had received my song and chapter called to tell me that she had been in tears every time she listened to that song and read the accompanying words. I realized from these points of feedback that no one could pay me enough money to do something other than this. By voluntarily giving value to others using the raw talents I had been blessed with, I was living squarely within my purpose. No corporate job or monetary rewards could compete with the spiritual high that I felt at that moment.

How can you compete against something one will gladly give away for free?

As a result of those strong feelings of fulfillment, I promptly quit a very high paying job that week, and renewed my determination to follow my dream with every ounce of focus I could muster. I knew that the combination of motivation, music, and mentorship was not necessarily a template for financial success, but it was who I am. This was my bliss, my life's purpose, my *must*. I was determined to *manifest my must*.

Measure Your Success

You can't improve what you can't measure. As such, I developed five measurable 'scorecard' factors to help me understand if my strategy was working or not, and I was happy to learn that my self-story was finally working.

The first point of measurement for me was that my **stakeholders** were showing me that their needs were being met. Unlike the previous job I held, I was actually providing a service that was simultaneously in line with my unique gifts, as well as the needs of a very specific group of people.

Second, my messaging and offerings were resulting in a **transformational** effect of influence on those stakeholders. There was no carrot and stick, no coercion, no sales job - just pure influence based on *their* needs, not mine.

Third, by creating these educational and entertainment products, I was finally implementing a business system – an **orchestration** of events that would ultimately produce residual income in the future without my having to always work physically for remuneration.

Fourth, I was using my own God-given **resources**, and playing roles that were within my talent zone. I was no longer a pretender to someone else's throne. Like Maximus, the general who became a slave in the movie *Gladiator*, I was finally taking off the mask, and answering my real name.

Fifth, and possibly most important, I recognized for myself the old saying that it is all up to "**you**" to decide how your story turns out. *No one but you can make your dreams come true.* I was taking full responsibility for my own outcomes.

The S.T.O.R.Y Strategy And Scorecard

These five factors form what I call the S.T.O.R.Y. strategy and scorecard for change. It contains all the ingredients needed for carrying out and measuring your success along the way: Stakeholder, Transformation, Orchestration, Resources, and You:

> **The S.T.O.R.Y. Strategy & Scorecard**
> - **S**takeholder
> - **T**ransformation
> - **O**rchestration
> - **R**esources
> - **Y**ou

Using this memorable scorecard process to write your story, you will be able to create success step by step, and keep track of your progress along the way.

You've probably noticed that these five strategic factors together spell the word S.T.O.R.Y. You've also probably noticed my use of the five 'C's to describe the patterns of your story, and later on, I'll use 'ABC' to describe the process of motivating and maintaining your self-story along the way. This is no coincidence. Besides my natural affinity for acronyms from years of management consulting, there is actually a well-researched reason for this approach. According to Dan and Chip Heath, authors of *Made to Stick*, the simpler an idea is to understand and remember, the easier it will be to implement in your life and business.

As such, I thought I'd make the ideas in this book very clear to 'C', simple as 'ABC', and full of narrative; after all, everyone loves a good 'S.T.O.R.Y.', right?

Story Assessment #6: Change

The change phase is where you take action against your mission statement – your future life and work goals – and measure your progress along the way:

No matter what 'most' people do, or what the norms are, you have your own special story. It may not be popular, or pragmatic, and it may not be expected, but it's *yours*, and that's what truly matters.

Write down the change you need to implement in your own story in order to get the results you seek:

_____

_____

_____

_____

_____

_____

As you pursue the change you seek, what specific *actions* will you take in order to capitalize on your strengths?

_____

_____

_____

As you pursue the change you seek, what specific things will you do less of in order to minimize your weaknesses?

_____

_____

_____

Change won't happen unless you have a burning, personal business case. *Why* are you willing to do the hard work involved in changing and pursuing my goals?

_____

_____

_____

_____

Using the S.T.O.R.Y. strategy and scorecard process, measure your progress:

Stakeholders:

Are you addressing the stakeholders who really need your service? Are you fulfilling their needs?

Transformation:

Are you leading and influencing your stakeholders based on *their* needs, or yours?

Orchestration:

Have you systematized your work processes so that they can work without you? Are you involving others in your processes?

Resources:

Are you utilizing your full, God-given talents? Are you expressing your creativity?

_____

_____

You:

Are you spending enough time to develop yourself further as a contributor or leader?

_____

_____

Who will you explain your desired changes to, and from whom will you periodically request feedback:

_____

_____

_____

_____

_____

_____

Okay, let's move on to the final two steps in writing your story – the conclusion and the contribution – the places where your greatness and potential will actually be manifested. Let's explore how you can immediately take control of your life and liberate the success and fulfillment that lie within you.

Ready? Let's go!

12.

Conclusion

One day your life will flash before your eyes.
Make sure it's worth watching.
– UNKNOWN

Whenever I'm out driving with my wife and children, we play car games, like 'I-Spy' and 'Slug-Bug'. We also like to sing songs like 'Bingo' and 'Zipiddy-doodah'. We do our fair share to try to fill up the time and keep the kids from getting bored, but no matter the distance, there's always one specific little question on their lips:

"Are we there yet?"

I'm ashamed to admit that I usually provide dispassionate responses like "we're close," or "almost there, honey!" – even if it's more like an hour to go. I liken this question to the one that so many of us ask about our own lives:

Am I successful yet?

Act four in your story – the conclusion – is when you can comfortably say, "I have arrived." However, it is not a place or a time that you arrive at, it is a *decision*. The answer to the question of whether or not you are 'there yet' is actually very simple, albeit counter-intuitive:

> You are a success the minute you abandon all
> distractions, make your decisions, and begin to take
> action toward your goals.

One of the biggest problems people face in life and at work is knowing *when* they've 'arrived'. Knowing when to be satisfied, content, and when to finally feel happy about where they are. Unlike the innocent car-question, not knowing when you're successful can cause plenty of problems, and for some, it can be downright disastrous. Also different from the car metaphor, success is more a set of choices, values and expectations, rather than a destination. If you expect certain things and don't get them, you may feel miserable even though others may see you as very successful according to their own expectations.

Less advanced societies seem to have developed ways of remaining perpetually happy and content – concepts the western world struggles with. Researchers have discovered that the happiest people on earth live in remote areas of Nigeria (BBC, 2003). These are people with no material wealth whatsoever, who simply wake up, and as long as the sun is in the sky, they proclaim: "today is a good day." What can we learn from these people?

> Now and then it's good to pause in our pursuit of
> happiness – and just be happy.
>
> – Guillaume Apollinaire

Live Your Dream Now

One of my favorite ways of explaining 'the conclusion' phase is the story of the two men who decided their dream was to live on a hill. One of them packed his belongings and immediately went to live on the nearest hill, while the other went off to drive a taxicab. When asked why he wasn't successfully living on the hill, the taxicab driver complained that it takes many years to save up enough money before you can afford the mortgage for the houses they build on the hill. He said he was driving a cab to save up money to someday live on the hill. He admitted he wasn't there yet.

His friend, on the other hand, declared himself a success, and walked off, smiling into the sun.

So in the end, one was living on a hill, and the other was working towards living on a hill. Which of these two was living their dream? Which one of them are you?

> You don't have to be great to get started; but you do have to get started to be great.
>
> – Les Brown

The other day I read a heartbreaking story in the newspaper about a scientist-turned-van driver who watched his contemporaries win the Nobel prize (MSNBC, 2008). Here's the story:

Alabama van driver headed to Nobel ceremony
Former scientist contributed to work done on gene research.

Associated Press: 12/04/08

HUNTSVILLE, Ala. - A scientist-turned-van driver in Alabama whose work helped two other men win this year's chemistry Nobel Prize is headed to Sweden to watch them collect the award. Douglas Prasher told The Huntsville Times he was flying to Stockholm on Thursday at the invitation of winners Martin Chalfie and Roger Tsien.

Prasher was a researcher in the 1980s when he isolated and copied a gene that makes some jellyfish glow green. His grant money ran out and he gave a copy of the gene to Chalfie and Tsien. Chalfie and Tsien won the $1.4 million prize for figuring out how to use the glow to study cells. A third scientist shared the award for discovering the protein in the 1960s.

The 57-year-old Prasher has struggled to find work as a biochemist and now drives a courtesy van for a Toyota dealership in Huntsville.

There is certainly nothing wrong in choosing another profession, if that is what this gentleman did. There is also nothing wrong in doing what you have to do in order to keep the lights on and food at the table. However, if you have a dream, hold on tight to it. Don't let it slip in favor of pragmatism. Live your dream now, no matter how little of it you can hold on to.

> The future doesn't lie ahead of you waiting to happen.
> It lies deep inside of you waiting to be discovered.
> - Unknown

Success Derailers

Why is it that so many people try so hard to achieve their success goals, but never seem to arrive? What is it that holds talented people back from the targets they seek?

The answer to this dilemma can be found in one word:

Derailers.

People who have been successful and can't figure out why they aren't 'getting ahead' are probably being derailed by some deeply entrenched values and motivations they aren't aware of – a blind spot in their lives. Derailers lodge themselves deep in our value systems, in our behavioral habits and preferences, and in the way we interact with people at an interpersonal level. To fully understand how derailers work, let us consider the metaphor of a vector.

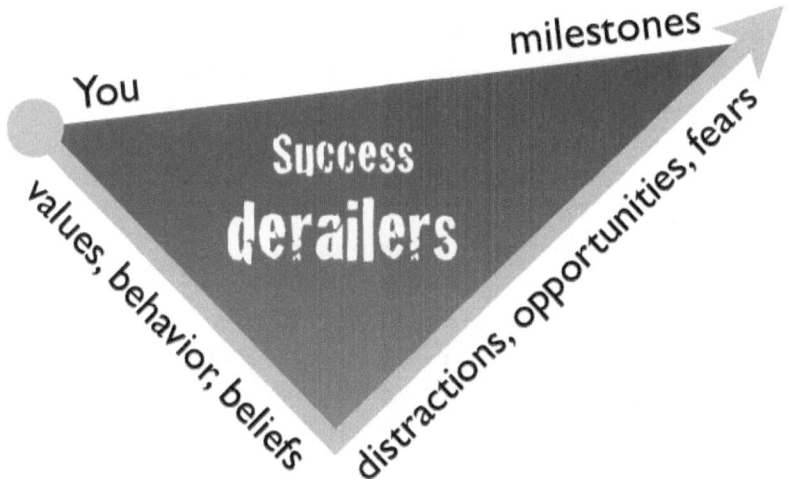

Imagine that you want to go from 'A' to 'B', or from "you" in the diagram, to certain success "milestones" in your plan. What goes wrong is that you find yourself derailed – diverted from your plan – by a combination of values, behavior, beliefs, tangents, opportunities, fears, and other distractions. The fastest way to go from where you are now to where you want to be is to be doing it RIGHT NOW. Not later, after you've triangulated through a myriad of other distractions, made your millions in another profession, or when you've won the lottery. Don't wait for your circumstances to change. Act now, and change your circumstances!

> Sometimes, little success is the enemy of big success.

Your actions speak much louder than your words. If you say that you want to live on a hill, don't go drive a taxi to make money so you can live on a hill. Go live on the hill today. If you say you are a writer, don't go to work as a carpenter so that you can someday make enough money to become a writer. Be a writer now. If you want to help others, don't wait until you are a millionaire before you start helping. Send whatever you have today, for there may not be another tomorrow.

The other day, I got a call from one of my former leadership development clients. He was practically in tears. His wife had left him, his business was in danger of bankruptcy, and he didn't know how he was going to provide for his three young children. He needed my help and counsel, and he needed it now.

I had a choice. I could help him, or I could say, "I don't help people anymore. I'm off driving a taxicab so I can someday make enough money to live my dream of helping people."

That wouldn't have made much sense, would it?

Of course I dropped everything, met him immediately for coffee, and offered him the best support and counsel I could give him. I did it because this is my purpose. I was placed on this planet so that I would be there when he called. I had no excuse but to show up, and there is nothing that will divert me from being here for him or any of my other clients. This is my dream, and I'm living it. This is my hill, and I refuse to wait until tomorrow to go live on it!

> **Don't let anyone divert you from your dream.**

Hold on – no matter what challenges come your way – and remind yourself what success really is:

1. Success is a series of choices you make to be in the *right* story for *your* life – not a destination you 'arrive' at.

2. Success is best defined by *you* – and no one else.

3. You are successful the moment you know your purpose, make your choices, drop all distractions, and begin to act.

There are those pragmatists for whom this approach may seem like 'happy-talk'. No doubt, for some, success has to be measured against tangible things, such as pay increases, promotions, income increases, client acquisitions, etc. There is certainly merit to the view that one should have 'achieved' something in order to feel accomplished.

To those who may struggle with the idea of following your purpose no matter what, I offer this question: is your dream really worth it to you? If your dream is not worth it, then by all means, don't pursue it. If your purpose is not strong enough, then you should certainly go do something else. But if your self-story is strong enough, convincing enough, and if you *must* manifest your must, then you will understand why there are no options when you decide to pursue your purpose. It's like diving off a cliff. Once you are airborne, the only option you have is to fall well into the water. You can't just press a button and stop the jump. There are no buttons in free-fall.

Feel, Be, Do, Have

You have probably heard a version of the following popular three-pronged progression for creating success: *thoughts beget actions, and actions beget results.* That progression is definitely true. Everything starts as a thought, and what you constantly think will ultimately manifest into what you do, which will in turn create results, whether positive or negative.

However, there is one construct that comes before thoughts – and that is *emotion*. Your emotions drive your feelings, which then drive your thoughts. Cutting-edge neuroscience is showing us the power of emotions over thoughts. Even though we are not consciously aware of what happens in our brains, it has been proven that when reacting to external stimuli, we first feel, and then we think. Before you can control your thoughts, you have to tap into your feelings.

> **We are feeling beings who think, not thinking beings who feel.**

The popular iceberg analogy is great for thinking about what constitutes the unconscious realm. Imagine your mind to be an iceberg with two categories, visible, and invisible. At the tip of the iceberg are those things you can see and control, such as actions and results; but hidden beneath the icy water, you have the things you can't easily see, let alone control, such as emotions, feelings and thoughts. This unseen realm actually has more power than the visible realm, and it is also the realm of potential derailers – those blind spots that can steal your dream. In order to better control your actions and results, you have to go down under the visible part of the iceberg, and deal with those powerful, invisible potential derailers – emotions, feelings, and thoughts. Emotional power comes from getting these invisible elements working for you, not against you.

The A.B.C. Of Emotional Power

The unseen power of emotion can either be obstacles or helpers, depending upon how you choose to handle it. Controlling your emotional power can be done using a process I call the 'ABC' of emotions. Your ability to unleash your personal, emotional power in support of your goals depends on your *attitude*, *belief*, and *care* within the emotional realm:

The ABC of EMOTIONAL POWER:
- **A**ttitude
- **B**elief
- **C**are

Attitude:

The first determinant – the 'A' of emotional power – is your **attitude**. Since we live in a highly interdependent world, your interpersonal skills and how you respond to situations are paramount to your success. Unfortunately, no one learns these critical skills in school, though research shows that above all else, in the 'real' world, your attitude is the greatest determinant of your altitude. Are you a positive thinker, or prone to skepticism? Are you sociable, or reclusive? Despite what most people thought they learned growing up, it turns out that simply getting along with people can be a more powerful positive force than raw talent, skills, or intelligence.

Belief:

The next determinant – the 'B' of emotional power – is an unshakable **belief** in yourself and your mission. If you believe in something, you will stay motivated, inspired, and carry with you a solid sense of *urgency* for success. If you believe, you'll be replacing fear with faith – and will go on even when the world says you can't. And finally, *if you believe*, there will be no unreachable goal, no impossible dream. Eventually, you will manifest your belief into actions that will deliver the results you seek.

Care:

The third determinant – the 'C' of emotional power – is how well you take **care** of your emotions. You must fortify and safeguard yourself from the constant distractions of toxic knowledge, situations, and relationships, so that your mission remains clear regardless of circumstances. You must regularly feed your soul the nourishment it needs to remain grateful, content, and fulfilled. Whatever process or language you use to connect, listen to, and live in harmony with your spirit and higher power, use it. Spend time alone with your spirit, drown out the voices of the world, and just listen to your own inner truth. Do whatever you can to hold onto your *faith* – for therein lies the final missing intangible for success and fulfillment.

Story Assessment #7: Conclusion

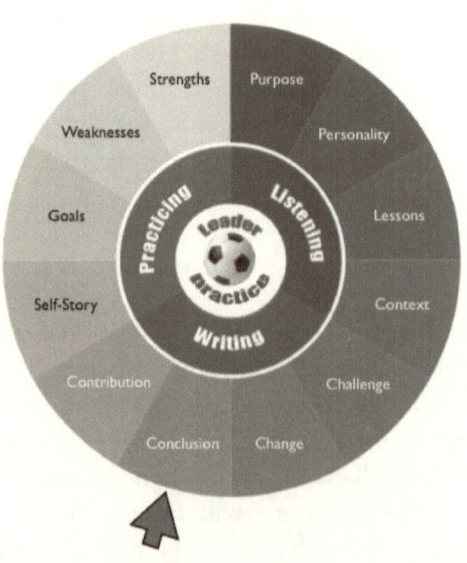

Visualize what your life would be like in the conclusion phase of your story. Write it down:

_____

_____

_____

_____

_____

Pretend that you are one of the two people in our earlier story whose dream was to live on a hill. Are you living on that hill today, or working at another job, (such as driving a taxicab), as a means of making enough money to eventually live on the hill?

_____

_____

_____

_____

_____

Write down three external derailers of which you should be careful.

_____

_____

_____

_____

Write down three derailers within your personality of which you should be aware.

Write down your plan to fortify yourself emotionally using the A.B.C. of emotional power:

Attitude:

What will you do to keep your attitude positive?

Belief:

What will you do to fortify and strengthen your belief in your own self-story and personal mission?

Care:

What will you do to take care of your dreams so that nothing can distract you?

I once worked with a colleague who had a most effective way of reminding himself that he had arrived at his successful career. Whenever he felt frustrated, he would roll his eyes, take a deep breath, and publicly remind himself that this was the vocation of which he had always dreamed. I could see that this affirmation always seemed to calm him down. It helped keep him at peace and in the moment.

Whatever works to remind you to be grateful for where you are and what you have, use it. Remember, emotional and spiritual peace is the ultimate conclusion – the 'happily ever after' – of any good story.

"Happiness is not a set of desirable life circumstances. It is a way of traveling."
– Ed Diener, PhD

13.

Contribution

Ask not what you can achieve. Ask what you can contribute.
– PETER DRUCKER

The part of folk stories that I enjoy the most is when you get to that 'aha' moment, and you hear, "and the moral of the story is ..." That's when you learn the crux of the story, the point of the parable, the overall lesson that should be learned from the story. Your story, like any other, should have a point. Something can be learned from your life, your choices, and your actions. One of the most powerful ways to design your story is to start with this question: if your story is being told when you're gone, what will the story teller say was the main point of your life, the moral of your story?

What will have been your *contribution*?

Tomorrow May Never Come

The following is an email letter I wrote one winter morning to all the people I had in my contact list. I was just inspired to share these words – completely out of the blue. Several years later, as I was writing this book, I read these words again, and found them surprisingly appropriate as advice for the contribution phase of one's success story.

At the time, I called the email, "Tomorrow May Never Come." Here it is:

Dear friends,

I was just this morning reading a magazine, where they were laying out the most recent, successful entrepreneurs who had made millions with little or no money in a short amount of time. Another magazine was profiling the careers of another set of very successful people in business, with new promotions to top leadership positions.

I was in awe of all the shiny, smiling, young, rich faces, until I turned a page, and the next smiling face in front of me was of someone who had just passed away. She was young, barely 36 years old, Harvard educated, already a Vice President at a major firm, and married with two children. But one day she came home and simply died – suddenly – and without warning.

All of a sudden, all the peer pressure I had been feeling a few minutes prior vanished, and my inspiration to write this email appeared in front of me like a welcome friend offering a cup of hot, smoldering java. I had to write this, regardless of how morbid it may sound to some of you. So, forgive me in advance....but here goes.

If you are one of the millions of people who wake up each day and wonder why they haven't reached their full potential, you are not alone. If you have ever read a magazine or watched TV and seen your peers in age and education who have achieved so much in terms of the appearances and trappings of success, and you've thought, "why not I?" - you are not alone. Most people think these thoughts at some point. "Why haven't I reached my full potential?" "Where am I in my journey?" "Did I take the wrong path?" "Why am I not rich, or more influential, or happier?"

However, if you have ever found yourself realizing that this thought process itself was ludicrous, and wondered why these things should even bother anyone in the first place, then you have started down the road to a very important healing in your life.

The ultimate personal freedom is achieved when you realize that all people, no matter their social, financial, educational, political achievements or stratification - are EQUAL. Yes! That means it is an exercise in futility to envy Bill Gates, or George Bush, or Obasanjo's son, or your neighbor who just became a millionaire last week, or your college classmate who just became the governor of your state at the ripe young age of 38. The reason peer pressure of any kind is a waste of time is simply this:

Tomorrow may never come.

A 100 year old man was once asked - what is the one thing you can say you truly enjoy about being this old? His reply was: "No more peer pressure!"

Don't act like you've never felt it. Peer pressure is all around us, but trust me on this one. As a long-time sufferer and member of the AAPPS (Association of Anonymous Peer Pressure Sufferers:-), I have researched and battled this issue until I found my own truth, which is this: none of these successful people will take any of their success with them to the grave. At that time, and at that hour, they, like you and I, will be lifeless, and their relevance will continue only in the minds of those they impacted and left behind. Neither fame nor political power are measures of success, because using those as metrics, Hitler would be every inch as successful as Gandhi.

In the larger scheme of life, all these outwardly "successful" people mean nothing more than the beggar on the street. To eradicate these worrisome thoughts that occasionally evade our mid-life minds, we have to look at the very source of peer pressure - competition in the childhood playground. Society has taught us to stratify ourselves, title ourselves, and judge ourselves based on external criteria. All this, when those external criteria are simply meaningless and temporary. And to make matters worse, we have carried these paradigms, as hidden ways of seeing the world, into adulthood.

So what criteria truly matter? How can we reprogram in our minds a return to the truth that was taken from us in the childhood playground? What criteria can we use to view ourselves so that we can feel a sense of progress, accomplishment, and contribution?

Those criteria, my friends, are met when you invest in human capital. Giving to others. Building others. Relationships. People. Not jobs, technology, cars, houses, or educational degrees. Those are just tools; the real work of human beings is being human. Helping people. Contributing to the value of life for others. Making things happen for others. Producing a smile on someone else's face other than your own. These are the things worth judging yourself by, and these are the things worth shaping your life, career, and aspirations by.

I am not proposing monk-hood or getting rid of all worldly possessions or aspirations. But I am proposing that we recommit ourselves to the importance of the human element. And why is this human element so much more important than everything else?

Because tomorrow may never come.

When acclaimed author Jim Collins (Good to Great) sought career advice from renowned management guru Peter Drucker, he asked something like this:

"What questions should one ask in determining what to do with one's life and career?" Drucker's reply was this:

"What will be your contribution?"

Stephen Covey said the same thing in his book, Seven Habits of Highly Effective People — but he put it another way ... "Begin with the end in mind." Friends, I'm sorry to break it to you, but life is ridiculously short. It will all be over soon, and you need to make the best of what you've been given by putting it in the service of others. In my opinion, your number one job is to create positive stories. You are here to create lasting, high quality stories for those you will leave behind when you are gone. At the end of this life, the only reward — the greatest reward — is the quality of the stories you leave in the minds of others.

So think about the relationships you have developed or are developing today. Will they leave good stories or a foul stench? If you haven't been thinking about life in this way, and you've made many relationship mistakes through "doing what you gotta do to survive" - don't worry. It's never too late. You can always start again and try to make things right. If some relationships in your life are not positive, fine; get rid of them. But do so quickly, gently, and kindly, and leave the best memory and story you possibly can in those people's minds.

Apologize to them for the things you've done, and show empathy regarding how you may have hurt them in that process; but move on, because you do not want to create more bad stories. Go away, start again, and begin working hard to create powerful and positive stories in the people you will meet anew. From now on, make everyone know how special he or she is, because they truly are. Empower the human element wherever you go.

It's just not worth it to gain the whole world, and leave bad stories. Make building great stories your number one priority:

Because tomorrow may never come.

Writing this was a risk for me. It is either a brave man or a fool who puts his thoughts out for others to judge. But I thought to myself — "ah, what the heck. Who am I fooling?" This is who I am. This is what I have to give, even if everyone else already knows it. This is my contribution, and I must contribute now.

You have greatness within you!

Pelè Raymond Ugboajah, PhD

Story Assessment #8: Contribution

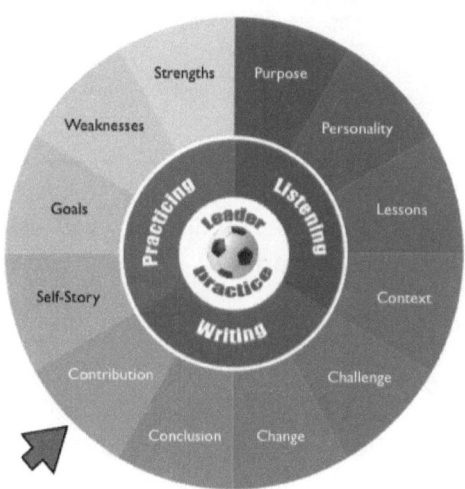

Now it is time to write down what your contribution will be. Start with the end in mind. What will be the crux of your story? What will be the moral of your story? Someday, when your story is told, the following will be the moral of that story – the *point* of your story:

_____

_____

_____

_____

_____

When your story is told, the following will have been your contribution to your family.

_____

_____

_____

_____

_____

When your story is told, the following will have been your contribution to the world of work.

_____

_____

_____

STORY-PRACTICING

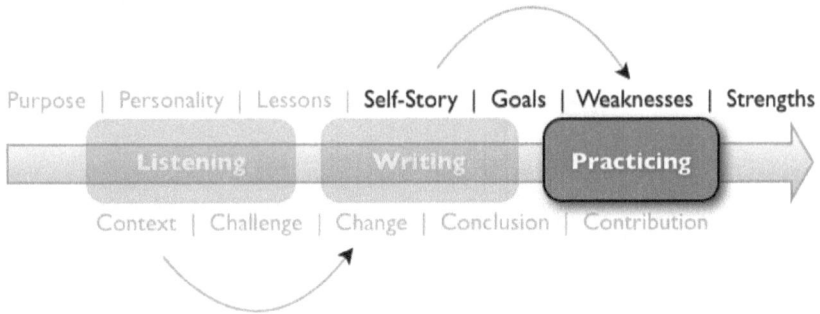

Purpose | Personality | Lessons | **Self-Story | Goals | Weaknesses | Strengths**

Listening | Writing | **Practicing**

Context | Challenge | Change | Conclusion | Contribution

W e have now reviewed the self-leadership skills of Story-listening and Story-writing. At this point you have begun to research your own story, to listen to your purpose and passions, and document your lessons. You have also written down specific, measurable actions that will be your schedule of events over the course of your new story. Now it is time to turn your vision into actions. To do this, you'll need to work with the following dimensions that you created or discovered during the Story-Listening and Story-Writing phases:

1. Self-Story
2. Goals
3. Weaknesses
4. Strengths

Over the course of this section, you will learn how to **'LeaderPractice'** your way to the success you seek. Using specific tools and analogies from the worlds of business, sports, and psychology, you will learn how to turn your intentions from conscious thought into automatic, unconscious action. Through 'practice' you'll learn how to enroll your mind – the most powerful force you have – in the service of your goals.

14.

Self-Story

Self-Image sets the boundaries of individual accomplishment.
– MAXWELL MALTZ

On May 6th, 1954, on a track in Oxford England, a young medical student was about to make sports history. It was widely believed on that day that it was impossible for a human being to run an entire mile in under four minutes. Doctors, scientists, and the public at large had long held this belief, and all records and experiments theretofore supported their position. And then came Roger Bannister. He almost missed the race on that day, but once he began running, a coordinated sprint with two of his teammates pushed him over the barrier. He ran a mile in 3 minutes, 59.4 seconds. At the time, his feat was considered to be one of the greatest sports achievements of all time (Academy of Achievement, 2008).

Fascinating as his run had been, Roger Bannister's record was soon eclipsed within a year by several other runners, who also broke the four-minute mile barrier, forever shattering the limiting belief that a human being could not run a mile in under four minutes.

What happened?

Certainly, the human body couldn't have evolved so rapidly in just one year! Or could it be that once Roger Bannister and other people started to believe that greater achievements were *possible*, they were able to aspire to and achieve greater goals? Could this be an example of 'mind over matter?'

The answer is yes. Your degree of belief has a lot to do with your degree of achievement.

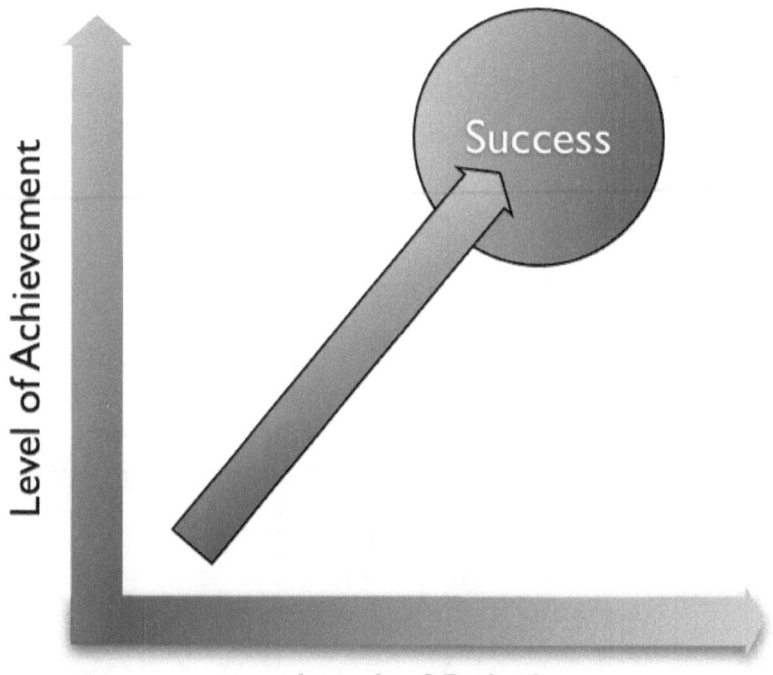

Human beings are born with a basic survival instinct, which in many ways, translates into a 'success mechanism' that works to guide them to whatever goals they deem most important. However, not everyone is fully in tune with this built-in success mechanism. Some people seem to have a greater 'knack' for pushing on and getting things done, while others are more passive, allowing circumstances to have their way more often than not. The major difference between these two kinds of people can be described along a continuum of how well conceived and compelling their self-stories are.

The person who has a compelling self-story, and believes she *can* do something, is much more likely to try it and do it than the person who simply believes she can't. In fact, the person who takes no action on account of their lack of belief is the only one who can expect a guaranteed result – failure.

Can you imagine the self-story that Mary Kay Ash told herself as she turned a $5,000 investment into a Billion dollar cosmetics business? Imagine the self-story that Ray Kroc must have told himself as he transformed himself from a fifty-two year old milk-shake machine salesman into the founder and builder of a global McDonald's fast food empire? Or can you imagine the kind of powerful, compelling, and unflinching self-story that Barack Obama must have repeated to himself as he battled from obscurity to the most grueling, most expensive, and most unlikely presidential victory in American history?

Most of us have heard the saying: 'if you can see it, you can be it'. But how can a person 'see' it? How do you decide, among all the other things you have to worry about in your busy life, that you are going to start 'seeing' all kinds of new, success possibilities?

Where do you start?

The answer lies is in how well you craft and deliver your self-story. The overall story that you burn into your mind can help to set all your success mechanisms into autopilot. Your job is simply to create that compelling self-story, and push it as deep and unforgettably into your mind as possible. You need to become an expert at saying, "Yes, I can!"

> When a person says 'yes', his gods also say 'yes'.
>
> – Igbo Proverb

How To Believe The Story Of You

The Self-Story I am talking about is the one you've been building throughout this book. By now, you should have a sense of your personality, what your purpose is, what you are passionate about, what your life lessons have been, and what your vision for the future is. You started with the end in mind, and have therefore laid out a story that can be told about you when you're gone – essentially, you now possess a blueprint of your life's plan going forward.

Now all you need to do is *believe* it!

I fully understand that it is difficult for some to just turn on faith like a water faucet. And I know that simply saying that something will be does not make it so. However, this is where the concept of *practice* comes in. LeaderPractice allows you to suspend your attempts at conscious belief, and through focused activity, train your unconscious mind to believe and do things for you.

Remember how my daughter learned to ride her bike? She certainly didn't believe she could do it. Consciously, she wasn't ready to 'see' the success that I saw for her. But through repetition and constant practice, her unconscious mind learned the process, and took over her tasks of bike-riding. Here's a series of steps for believing in the story of you:

1. Learn from proven success processes
2. 'Practice' your success story until it becomes a 'habit'
3. Implement your story with faith and conviction.

First you need to find models of the success you seek – people who have already achieved what you're hoping to achieve. Learn how they did what they did, and like Roger Bannister and others who beat the four-minute mile, you'll be able to find the confidence to reach higher.

> Study the success processes of others who have done what you seek to do. Gain confidence from knowing that if they can do it, so can you.

Next, you need to repeat your future success story to yourself on a daily basis. You need to write it down and paste it strategically in places where you can see it. And you need to tell (only) *trusted* friends or family about it. By constantly marketing, selling, and repeating your self-story to yourself, you will wake up one day, and just like my daughter, you will have found powerful new belief skills, ready and at your service.

You'll have started to believe in yourself.

> **Believe and act as if it were impossible to fail.**
> – Charles F. Kettering

I remember once when I had a serious lapse in my own self-belief. I experienced this phenomenon – the lack of a compelling self-story – when I worked for Les Brown, one of the world's most renowned motivational speakers. He had given me the task of consolidating and implementing all of his marketing and outreach efforts. At the same time, he offered me the unique opportunity to shadow him and even speak alongside him at certain events. For me, this was the opportunity of a lifetime! But something was missing. I was there in full mind and body, but my spirit was lagging behind because I didn't believe in myself. I couldn't imagine that I too could ever become a successful speaker, and I was therefore not willing or able to take the risks necessary to achieve my goals.

One day, Les and I were on the phone and I was complaining as usual. At a certain point, he stopped me and said: "when I was your age, I never had a Les Brown I could pick up the phone and call at a moment's notice. And even if there was someone I looked up to, they certainly didn't have any time for me."

I was humbled and silent, as he continued.

"You need to replace your fear with faith. You are a talented young man – more than many – and with unlimited potential. But your negative self-talk is stopping you from moving forward."

I jumped in, and asked him how he keeps himself positive. His response was that it all comes down to the quality of your self-talk.

He told me he has a special poem, (written by Berton Braley), which he recites to himself on a regular basis whenever doubts step in:

If you want a thing bad enough
To go out and fight for it,
To work day and night for it,
To give up your time and your peace and your sleep for it

If all that you dream and scheme is about it
And life seems useless and worthless without it

If gladly you'll sweat for it,
Fret for it,
Plan for it,
Lose all your terror of the opposition for it,

If you'll simply go after that thing that you want
With all your capacity,
Strength and sagacity,
Faith, hope and confidence, and stern pertinacity,

If neither cold poverty, famished and gaunt,
Nor sickness nor pain
Of body or brain
Can keep you away from the thing that you want,

If dogged and grim you besiege and beset it,
With the help of God,
You'll get it.

(Braley, 1916).

Only years later did I realize what he was doing. This wasn't just some 'positive thinking' stunt – he had this process down to a science! By repeating these words every single day, he was actually practicing the neural 'muscles' in his unconscious mind. He was fortifying his mind with emotional power, faith, and belief systems that he knew he could not achieve at a conscious, logical level. He was feeding his mind the power of faith in a compelling self-story – the food of success!

I took his advice, and repeated those same words everyday as I went about my goals. I also crafted a compelling self-story and repeated it to myself on a daily basis. At the time, my goal was to join Toastmasters and gain confidence as a speaker. I did that. My next goal was to enter some of the Toastmasters competitions. I did that. My next goal was to win a humor competition, and I did that as well. The first year, I competed in every competition I possibly could, and the following year I won the entire District 6 International Championship of Public Speaking.

Thanks to Les Brown, who believed in me when I didn't believe in myself, I was able to break my own four-minute mile. Now I feel unstoppable. My confidence is secure, and there is not a shred of doubt in my mind that whatever I put my mind to will someday come to pass. I finally learned to believe my own self-story!

LeaderPractice Your Self-Story

I draw no distinctions between what it takes to practice your physical muscles, your mind, and your leadership behavior patterns. They all work like habits – unconsciously and automatically. My daughter no longer 'thinks' about riding her bike, she just does. When I play the piano, I don't consciously 'think' about where my fingers are going with an arpeggio. When you talk, you don't consciously 'think' about how your tongue needs to curl to produce each word. When I give a speech, I no longer 'think' about all the gestures, eye contact strategies, and timing cues that I once had to work so hard on in my Toastmasters days. And yet, we do all these things because – through practice – we've become very excellent at doing them at an unconscious level.

> We are what we repeatedly do.
> Excellence then, is not an act, but a habit. - Aristotle

Here's an example from my self-story:

Context:

My purpose is to use my God-given talents to help others find and use theirs. I am an outgoing personality, very sociable and creative. My biggest challenges have been my fear of failure and skepticism. The most important lessons in my life are lessons about the importance of family, and the importance of innovation and entrepreneurship.

Challenge:

In my personal life and business, I have a strong sense of urgency regarding creativity. Art, Music, Writing, and Speaking are the major vehicles through which this creativity will occur. The purpose of my creativity is to convey a message to people that will teach and enlighten them on topics relating to personal and leadership development as well as the pursuit of fulfillment, success, and significance in their lives and businesses.

Change:

In order to live my purpose, I will create and develop a firm called LeaderPractice – a leadership development company focused on helping individuals find their purpose, design their future, and live out their success – without abandoning any of my unique talents of motivation, music, and mentorship. I am committed to using all of my God-given talents in the pursuit of providing value in the business world.

In my family, I am committed to maintaining and enjoying the love and friendship of my wife and life partner. I am committed to passing along positive values and providing guidance to my young children so that they can navigate this difficult world with more support than I received in my younger years. I am committed to family. I love watching my family grow.

In my relationships, I am committed to keeping reciprocal, drama-free friendships alive and well. I am committed to bi-directional relationships where I receive value and provide it to my friends at the same time. With everyone I know I will portray the positivity that I seek. I will work hard to remove toxic people from my life, and to encourage only those relationships that provide positive energy and spiritual growth.

I am committed to pursuing a healthy life. Exercise, good eating habits, and good mental habits are all part of my plan to maintain a stable and positive outlook.

In my finances, I am committed to the idea of earning income both as wages, and in a residual manner. It is my goal to develop both an active and a passive income stream from my work. While I strive for innovation, I will also work hard to be interdependent and collaborative with others as part of a larger team for business success.

Conclusion:

I am living my dream today. Success for me looks like I am using all my creative gifts, music, writing, and speaking, in the service of my purpose. My family is whole, healthy, and happy. I am healthy. I am earning money from wages, and I am also earning money from residual income. Nothing shall distract me from this stated purpose.

Contribution:

When my story is told, let it be said that I was a 'maker' of things through art, music, and literature; that I cared deeply about people; and that I left none of my God-given talents unused in the fulfillment of my life's purpose. Let it be said that I helped others find their life's purpose, even as I found mine.

Story Assessment #9: Self-Story

Now the time has come to write your Self-Story. This is what all of our worksheets and questions so far have been preparing you for. Starting with your purpose, and based on all the information you've collected so far, use the five acts structure to organize and summarize you're the Story Of You:

Context: (purpose, personality, and lessons)

Challenge: (opportunities, and urgency for change)

_____

_____

_____

_____

_____

_____

Change: (what actions you will take in different areas of life)

_____

_____

_____

_____

_____

_____

Conclusion: (starting with the end in mind, what success looks like for you)

_____

_____

_____

_____

_____

_____

Contribution: (what you will given to the world)

_____

_____

_____

_____

_____

_____

Now, read your self-story once a day. Remember that this is a living document, meaning it should evolve as you do. Paste a copy of it strategically in places where your eyes will find it at home and at work. Do this for at least a month. Very soon, every single word in your mission statement will be adopted by your unconscious powers and you'll be on your way to a successful implementation of the story of you.

15.

Goals

When you want something, all the universe conspires in helping you to achieve it.
– PAULO COELHO

S occer is the most popular game in the world, and it is known in most places outside the United States as 'football, the beautiful game'. The game is exactly that – beautiful – but for me it holds an additional, special significance. Soccer has become for me a metaphor for achieving goals in life and work. Imagine that you are a *team of one*, and your objective is to achieve certain goals. Let's review three reasons why soccer might be a useful metaphor for setting and achieving those goals:

Opponents

First, the object of soccer is to score goals, but like most games, scoring is not done in a vacuum – you have to score those goals despite an *opponent* who is actively playing against you. In life, people tend to set goals and pursue them *without* paying enough attention to the derailers and opponents that are actively working against them.

Different Roles

Second, you can't score goals with just one player. You need several players working together, each with a *different* role. When most people set goals, they do so without assigning different roles to the tasks that comprise the main goal. For example, an obvious derailer to any goal is one's health. As such, if one's goal is to create wealth, you need other tasks, (or players), assigned specifically with maintaining your health so that you are able to enjoy the wealth in the end.

Balance

Third, in soccer you score goals best when there is a clean division of labor, and no one player *holds onto the ball* for too long. In life, you have to be balanced in terms of your focus on the various goals and tasks you tackle. Too much focus or neglect in any one area could harm your overall balance, and lead to ineffectiveness in the pursuit of your overall goal.

Think of your overall goal as the opponent's goalpost, and your players as the smaller tasks that comprise your main goal. Let's take a look at how the game uses your players (tasks) to score goals.

Each team has eleven players that fall into three groups, each with a clear set of priorities. The players nearest to the opposing team are the *strikers*, and their job is simply to score goals. They never venture too far backward, and always keep themselves at the ready to do their job. The next group is the *midfielders*, and their main task is to dispossess the opposition of the ball, and create new possession opportunities for the team. And finally, there are those players who are closest to the team's goalpost. These are the *defenders*, and their job is to prevent opponents from scoring a goal, or getting too close to the goalkeeper. Last but not least, is the goalkeeper, who is the last person standing between the opponents and a goal.

The 'players' are tasks that contribute to your larger goal, and their overall objective is to help you achieve that primary goal. Instead of just creating those tasks, you could put them into categories, and give them separate, specific functions, so that together, they would act like a team of players. They would all work together, but they would do so by fulfilling different roles as you move toward your ultimate primary goal.

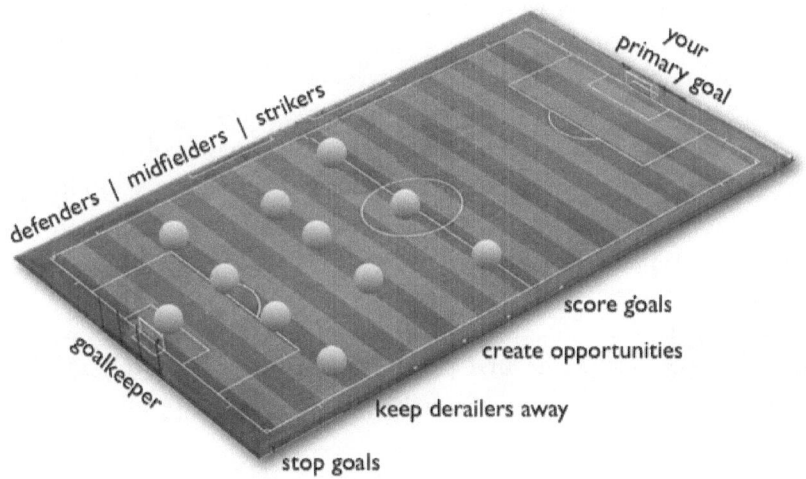

In the soccer metaphor, the goalkeeper is your conscious mind – your final decision-maker, gatekeeper and protector. Your defenders are the sub-tasks you are going to create in order to keep all negative derailers, weaknesses, self-doubts, fears, and toxic people out of your way. Your mid-fielders are going to be more sub-tasks, which you will design to help you seek out circumstantial challenges that you can turn into opportunities. And finally, your strikers are the sub-tasks most closely related your end-goal.

The traditional goal-setting process most people are used to features a rather linear approach, which does not take into account the reality of your *opponents*, which are constantly 'playing' against you at all times. Not only do you need to create forward momentum toward your primary goals, you also need to fend off these opponents, turn disadvantages into advantages, stop oncoming challenges in their tracks, and prevent derailment from goals scored against you. When it comes to setting and achieving goals, you need a *team* of tasks working together.

The Team Of You

Several years ago, I attended a training event in Las Vegas, Nevada. The main highlight from that training, and the most enjoyable, was when the entire class went outdoors and was divided up into two teams so that we could play a game to reinforce some of the business training that we had received. I was amazed at how business concepts sunk in so much faster and better when a game analogy revealed the truth behind them. That was probably when I first experienced the powerful similarities between games and life.

Imagine again that you are a 'team of you', and your players (your sub-tasks) are all working toward scoring (your primary goal) for you. Let's take a look at how the soccer team analogy might work using a real life example. Let's say your primary goal is to become a musician. The first thing you might do is write yourself a broad primary goal or mission statement that will support your self-story:

> *"I will become a fulltime musician. I have the competence, desire, and determination to persevere in this chosen profession."*

Now, if you were going about this the traditional way, you might consider writing out a linear list of all the sub-tasks that will support your ultimate goal of being a musician, such as:

1. I will begin practicing for two hours daily
2. I will advertise for band members

3. I will attend auditions at hiring bands
4. I will seek out opportunities to watch and learn from others
5. I will download my favorite songs and learn how to play them
6. I will buy a new piano and guitar

Notice that all of these sub-tasks are linearly focused in one direction. They are all serving the singular purpose of getting you closer to 'scoring' your ultimate goal of becoming a musician.

But something is missing here.

What about the 'opponents' that are playing against you? What about all the potential obstacles, both internal and external, that will surely come your way?

In the above example, we have not planned out any consistent activities that will prevent your opponents from slipping past you, and there will be many of them, such as procrastination, behavioral derailers, toxic people, and unforeseen distractions you may not even be able to imagine at this time.

We also have not placed any consistent activities into your task mix that will take unforeseen circumstances and turn them into new advantages. Finally, you have no goalkeeper to protect you, and whatever new beliefs, doubts, or fears are injected into your mind, will be free to operate on you.

Can you see how this could be a recipe for disaster?

You would proceed with the very best of intentions, but you could easily find yourself derailed and cut short in your tracks by both internal and external factors. What you need is a 'team of you' that has tasks subdivided into multiple functions, some scoring, some defending, and some creating new opportunities for scoring.

Consider the following distribution of sub-tasks using the soccer metaphor:

MAIN GOAL - To Become a Musician:

SUB-TASKS:

1. Striker tasks: (directly related to the main goal)
    a.   I will buy a new piano and guitar.
    b.   I will begin practicing for two hours daily.

    c.   I will advertise for band members.

    d.   I will attend auditions at hiring bands.

    e.   I will seek out opportunities to watch and learn from others.

    f.   I will download my favorite songs and learn how to play them.

    g.   I will buy a new piano and guitar.

2. Midfielder tasks: (indirect - for creating new opportunities)

    a.   I will create balance in my life by setting sub-tasks in other areas, such as my family, finances, spirituality, and physical fitness.

    b.   I will read 'How to Win Friends and Influence People' to fortify my interpersonal skills.

    c.   I will indentify both short and long-term goals to make sure all of my sub-tasks are integrated and congruent.

3. Defender tasks: (for stopping opponents in their tracks)

    a.   I will work out daily and eat well to maintain my health.

    b.   I will develop a system to avoid people who tell me I can't achieve my goals.

    c.   I will write down and recite my goals daily as positive affirmations.

    d.   I will make only S.M.A.R.T. goals (specific, measurable, attainable, realistic, time-based).

4. Goalkeeper: (for making sure no goals are scored against you)

    a.   I will fortify my mind, and keep it safe from invading thoughts, doubts, and lack of self-belief.

    b.   I will affirm daily that positivity, persistence, and perseverance are my greatest armor against failure.

Following is a template for helping you delegate striker, midfielder and defender roles to your sub-tasks:

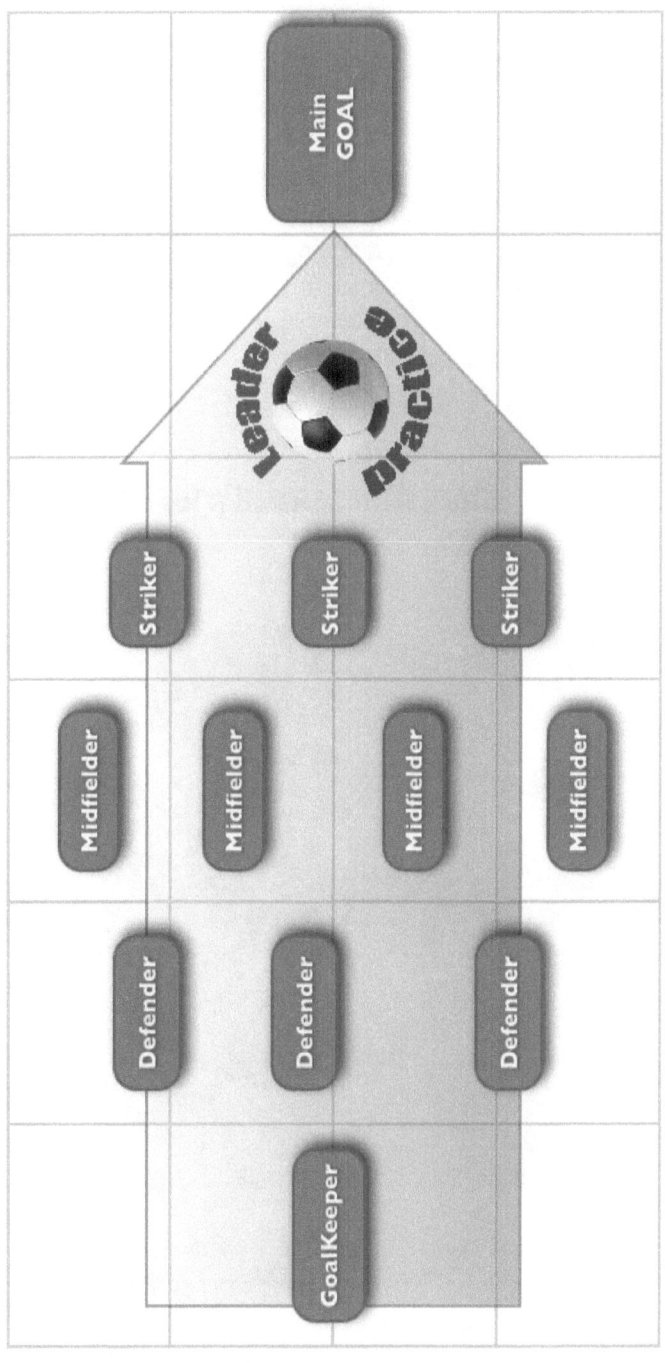

Using the soccer metaphor, here now are three basic suggestions for dealing with goals:

1. Break large goals into smaller, manageable sub-tasks (players).
2. Give those sub-tasks separate functions, such as (a) strikers getting you closer to your end goal, (b) midfielders converting challenging situations into new opportunities, and (c) defenders stopping derailers and opponents to your goals.
3. Write down all the goals and sub-tasks you come up with, and 'practice' them everyday.

Story Assessment #10: Goals

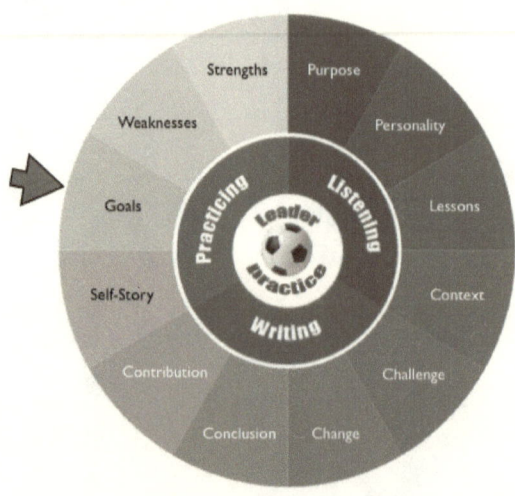

Write down one of your primary goals:

_____

_____

Now write down the sub-tasks that will support your primary goal. Arrange them into three categories. Strikers are those sub-tasks that are directly related to your primary goal. Midfielders are those sub-tasks that are designed to help you take advantage of existing or unforeseen challenges and turn them into opportunities and advantages. Defenders are those sub-tasks designed to keep you aware of, and defend you from opponents that are working against you, trying to derail you from outside, as well as inside.

Strikers:

_____

_____

_____

_____

_____

_____

Midfielders:

_____

_____

_____

_____

_____

Defenders:

The 'Team of you' approach will help you get past the opponents – the derailers and procrastinations that stop so many of us from reaching our goals. It is well documented that the best way to learn something is by actually doing it. As such, you can be sure that if you are ever in a coaching class of mine, we'll be out on the field, playing soccer as a way of practicing and reinforcing these self-leadership concepts. As I like to say – *you can't learn to play soccer at a seminar!* ™

16.

Weaknesses

The acknowledgment of our weakness is the first step in repairing our loss.
– THOMAS À KEMPIS

The leadership development field has gone the way of most of psychology. It has become too concerned with discovering weaknesses to be fixed as opposed to strengths to be celebrated and leveraged. In my early days as a leadership development consultant, I noticed a clear bias in the inquiry materials toward seeking out weaknesses in leaders. Almost like 'elimination' psychology, except that the output reports were glossed over with very flowery positive language to mask the true nature of the hunt. On the surface, not too many people are complaining about this, because organizations pay well for psychologists to help diagnose problems and 'fix' their people – or recommend those that should be promoted or removed altogether.

Even though most organizations start out with shiny brochures touting various leadership competencies, when it comes to actually selecting and developing people, they, like psychologists, often default to a search for 'what's wrong' instead of 'what's great' about people.

So what's wrong with that? If it ain't broke, why fix it?

I understand that argument, but I think that there are related performance and quality consequences that should not be ignored. If you start from weaknesses, you'll continue to focus attention on them, and the result will be a self-defeating cycle. You'll get what you look for. However, if we proactively listen to people's stories, in search of what's great about them, we will expose ourselves, and our organizations, to a whole new set of possibilities.

Consider the role of Human Resources as a profession. Why is it that people dread the entrance of the HR executive? Or why is it that people are afraid when called in for a psychological assessment, or a performance review? Furthermore, why is it that all those assessments come across as 'trick' questions? Is someone trying to play 'gotcha' psychology with your career?

Unfortunately, this is the state of the art today.

Thankfully, there is hope on the horizon. A new form of psychology has now been introduced by the likes of Martin Seligman and Jonathan Haidt. This new approach is called 'positive' psychology' and it seeks first to find what is great about people, and then leverage those strengths vigorously. The narrative, story-driven approach lends itself well to positive psychology's methods of inquiry because people are much more open to talking about their stories when they know that the stories 'won't be used against them'.

In the end, the key to successful leadership development is balance – to search a person's story as hard for strengths as you might for weaknesses, and practice leveraging them as hard as you might practice eliminating 'development challenges'.

Develop a Desire for Change – Publicly

The main output of Story-Listening is that you will understand three things about yourself: (a) your purpose, (b) your lessons learned, and (c) the strengths and weaknesses that are inherent to your personality. By knowing your personality strengths, you have a good sense of what you should do more of, as you move toward your goals. Similarly, by knowing your weaknesses, (or development opportunities as some may prefer to call them), you know what to do less of. Here's an example. Let's say you learn from a combination of psychological tests, and your own observations that you have a tendency toward skepticism. That may or may not qualify as a development opportunity for you, but if it does, you could take the following steps:

- Try to monitor your thoughts and find out what *triggers* the behavior you wish to minimize.
- Propose a different behavior to replace the old 'weakness'.
- Once you've isolated the trigger for the behavior you consider a weakness, you can recognize it coming, and proactively act to replace it with a different response.

This balance of doing more with your strengths, and manifesting less of your weaknesses is a well-known approach to leadership development. However, it is not enough, because for the most part, it can sometimes be a cosmetic and superficial approach to change.

People don't change just because you tell them to.

The desire to change can only come from the subject. It can't be given to them. They have to want it for themselves.

How then does a person increase their strengths and reduce their weaknesses? The answer is that they have to develop a burning, *public* desire to change. It can't be comfortable, and it can't be completely private. The subject must announce to a trusted party that they intend to change, and have that person help to hold them *accountable* to their commitment.

Urgency is one of the first things required in any meaningful change. That urgency can't be manufactured. It has to be real. If a person has a strong, built in desire to power through something, their chances of success are magnified. Here are three steps to leverage trusted third parties in your change process:

1. Tell certain trusted people about the weaknesses you want to work on.
2. Get their feedback. Are those the weaknesses they see? If not, learn more from them until you arrive at a consensus of development areas.

3. Take action. Along the way, ask for feedback from the people you've chosen so that you can get a sense of whether or not they see any progress in the behavioral dimensions you're working on.

By making your efforts to grow as a person and as a leader are made public, you increase your sense of urgency, knowing that those people are watching, and will hold you accountable along the way.

Story Assessment #11: Weaknesses

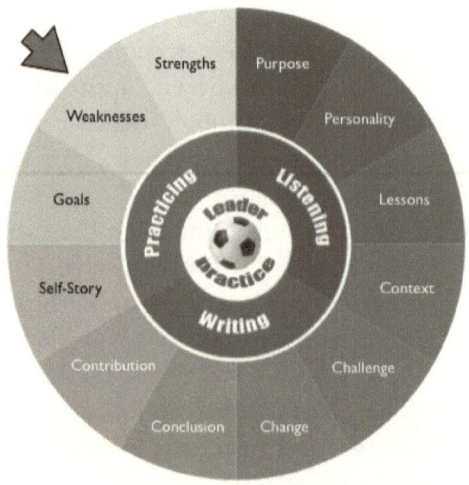

What are your weaknesses?

_____

_____

_____

_____

What consequences are these weaknesses producing in your life?

What will you do to minimize these weaknesses?

Whom will you declare your plans to for support and feedback?

17.

Strengths

Let me tell you the secret that has led me to my goal.
My strength lies solely in my tenacity.
– LOUIS PASTEUR

In 2003, Aron Ralston found himself literally between a rock and a hard place. He had been climbing the remote peaks of Blue John Canyon in Utah, when his right arm became trapped under a boulder. He hung on for days, hoping for help to come, but none came. When asked later how he handled the pain, he said: "I felt the pain and I coped with it. I moved on."

In his book, *Between a Rock and a Hard Place,* Ralston describes how he held on for days despite his hunger and dehydration. He ended up drinking his own urine, carving his name on the rocks, and videotaping his final goodbyes in case his body was found later on.

What kept him alive?

Emotional tenacity.
So far we've talked about how success is determined by your ability to create and deliver a compelling self-story. Now let's take a look at how success is also determined by your spirit of tenacity. In life, the race is not won by the most talented, or the strongest, but rather, by the most tenacious.

Regardless of your strengths, nothing works without emotional tenacity and the will to persevere.

William Wallace of Braveheart was driven by tenacity and perseverance. Okonkwo of Things Fall Apart was driven by passion and tenacity. Jesus persevered until the end. Martin Luther King was driven by a tenacious commitment to freedom and equality for all. These virtues come from the intangible conductor of your life's orchestra: the tenacity of your spirit.

Have you ever felt down and out? Have you ever felt like you'd lost your will to persevere? Have you ever felt like you just couldn't find the core motivation to go on? If you've ever felt these emotions, it was because your spirit was not congruent with your evolving story and strategy for success.

You were experiencing a misalignment of motivation and mission, and you were struggling with your will to persevere.

In order to achieve your goals, you have to *believe* again – innocently and passionately – just like you once did at the beginning of your story. You have to ignite your soul with the sense of urgency necessary to achieve your strategy – no matter what obstacles might come your way. And you have to constantly remember *why* you must achieve your goals. Most importantly, you have to persevere.

> "Nothing in the world can take the place of persistence. Talent will not; nothing in the world is more common than unsuccessful men with talent. Genius will not; unrewarded genius is a proverb. Education will not; the world is full of educated derelicts.
>
> Persistence and determination alone are omnipotent."
>
> *– Calvin Coolidge*

Story Assessment #12: Strengths

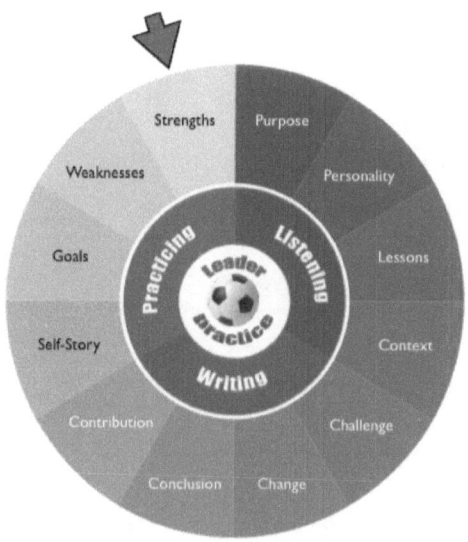

What are your strengths?

_____

_____

_____

_____

What advantages do your strengths produce in your life?

_____

_____

_____

_____

_____

What will you do to maximize these strengths?

_____

_____

_____

_____

To whom will you declare your plans for support and feedback?

_____

_____

_____

_____

Epilogue

Twenty years from now you will be more disappointed by the things that you didn't do than by the ones you did. So throw off the bowlines. Sail away from the safe harbor. Catch the trade winds in your sails. Explore. Dream. Discover.
– MARK TWAIN

Several college campuses across the United States hold annual events that have come to be known as 'last lectures'. In these talks, professors are invited to consider what they would teach their students if they had one last chance to do so before their demise. During these events, the wisdom being shared takes on a special meaning and urgency due to the hypothetical time limit placed on the lecturer's life. On September 18th, 2007, professor Randy Pausch got his chance to participate in this annual tradition, and he used it to give an enthusiastic

lecture to four hundred observers at Carnegie Mellon University. But what made this particular event so spectacular is that it was not a hypothetical last lecture. It was the real thing. This was in fact his *final* lecture. Randy Pausch had just been diagnosed with terminal pancreatic cancer and given only six months to live.

Faced with the reality of his imminent demise, he decided to give a final lecture titled, '*Really Achieving Your Childhood dreams*'. In that lecture, he talked about the importance of having dreams, achieving dreams without fear, and living your dreams. In his final few months after the lecture, he set out to achieve a list of his own childhood dreams, such as playing football with the Pittsburgh Steelers, and going on a trip to Disneyland with his family. In the end, his goal was to do his best to leave a legacy of wisdom for his children. When asked by Diane Sawyer of ABC News about how he felt knowing that his last lecture had already been seen by more than ten million people around the world, he answered thus: "That lecture was only designed for three people – my kids." He died on July 25th, 2008.

Given the chance, what would be the topic of *your* last lecture?

I have learned that success is to be measured not so much by the position that one has reached in life as by the obstacles which he has overcome while trying to succeed.

- Booker T. Washington

There is a lot of daylight between 'once upon a time', and 'lived happily ever after'. *The Story Of You*, like anything else, will take some focused introspection and work. This process is not by itself a panacea. However, you can count on one thing. If you plan the story of you in advance, develop it, and execute it, you'll get results that are vastly superior to what you would get if you did nothing at all. So square your shoulders, stand firm, find your purpose, and create your future – *today*!

"At every crossroad, follow your dream.
It is courageous to let your heart lead the way." – LELAND THOMAS

The song below is my gift to you.

Be well.

Tomorrow, I will find myself a rainbow
Take me to that pot of gold, in my mind, I will find

Tomorrow, take me where I really want to go
Let me reap what I have sown, I'll take a stand, faith in hand

Tomorrow, I might not make it to the day, when my story's told
But someone else might find their way, 'cos I walked this road
In the end, what matters most
Is I'll be the best that I can be today

Tomorrow, give me just one more chance to show
I can let go of the sorrow, of yesterday, and keep my faith in ...

Tomorrow

© Pele Raymond Ugboajah, PhD
(You may download this song from www.LeaderPractice.com)

THE STORY WORKBOOK

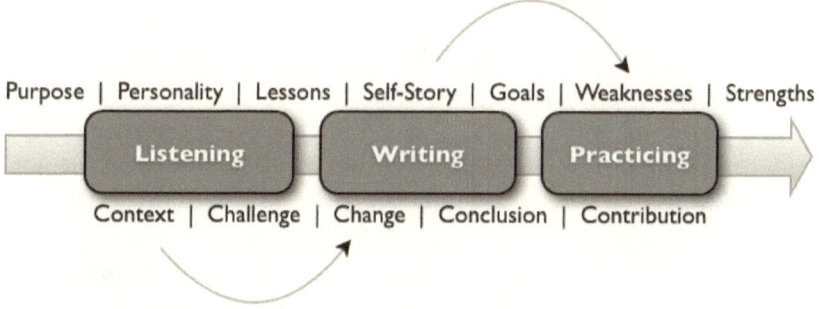

ongratulations! You've arrived at the Story Workbook! This is where we will take advantage of all the concepts and processes that you've learned so far and use them to navigate through the creation of *your* story. Here's the gist of what we've covered so far:

1. There is positive power in your personal narrative, but you can't find it unless your proactively seek it. Not only does 'story' have a transformative, influential power when told to others, it can play a powerful role in changing our own lives. By creating a compelling and influential 'self-story', we can change the course of our lives, and begin to live a life of design, rather than by default. Most important, there is power and uniqueness in *your* story, which you must discover and use as the springboard for your future success.

2. Once you are crystal clear on your story, you have to use a certain technology to activate the belief and goal-striving mechanisms within you, which will see you through to the success you seek. This technology is called LeaderPractice, a process that is based on the neuroscience of how we learn, change, and develop habits. By taking advantage of the

inherent powers in both your conscious and unconscious minds, you are able to push yourself to achieve far greater levels of success than you ever imagined.

3. The *Story of You* requires that you start with the end in mind. By simply asking the question, "what will be the story told about me when I am gone?" you are well on your way to designing the outcomes you seek. You can then begin a process of Story-Listening, in which you seek to understand your purpose, your personality, and your lessons learned. With this 'story assessment', you can then begin Story-Writing your future success by using a framework that is taken from the way the greatest stories on earth are made and told. Finally, to reinforce and implement your newly minted success story, you can rely on Story-Practicing to help create powerful new success habits that will guide you to accomplish your goals.

Your Self-Scoring Story Assessment

The following self-scoring assessment will help you start thinking about who you've been, who you are, and who you want to be going forward. By doing this rudimentary assessment, you will gain a cursory idea of the areas that may need more of your attention as you create the new story of you.

> Contact LeaderPractice for information about a more detailed Story Assessment process.

On the following pages, using your best judgment, read each statement, and then provide an answer regarding your level of agreement with it on the scale on the right. (1 being very low agreement, 5 being neutral, and 10 being extremely high agreement).

Your Story Assessment

STORY-LISTENING

PURPOSE

I would be doing exactly what I am doing today if I were given $20 million and 10 years to live.	1	2	3	4	5	6	7	8	9	10
I am currently 'living my dream'.	1	2	3	4	5	6	7	8	9	10
I am passionate about my work.	1	2	3	4	5	6	7	8	9	10
The work that I do greatly utilizes my personal	1	2	3	4	5	6	7	8	9	10

strengths and skills.										
PERSONALITY										
I am aware of my personality strengths and weaknesses.	1	2	3	4	5	6	7	8	9	10
I am aware of what others see as my personality strengths and weaknesses.	1	2	3	4	5	6	7	8	9	10
I consciously do a little each day to maximize my strengths and minimize my weaknesses.	1	2	3	4	5	6	7	8	9	10
LESSONS										
I am not currently relearning any lessons I have already learned in my life so far.	1	2	3	4	5	6	7	8	9	10
I have written down all the major lessons my life has uniquely taught me.	1	2	3	4	5	6	7	8	9	10
STORY-WRITING										
I have mapped out my self-story in terms of context, challenge, change, conclusions, and contribution.	1	2	3	4	5	6	7	8	9	10
I have a good sense of what my story will be when others someday tell it.	1	2	3	4	5	6	7	8	9	10
I am clear on what my intended contribution will be.	1	2	3	4	5	6	7	8	9	10

STORY-PRACTICING										
I regularly practice my self-story until success becomes a series of automatic habits in my life.	1	2	3	4	5	6	7	8	9	10
I am clear about what my goals are and I have created sub-goals to support them.	1	2	3	4	5	6	7	8	9	10
I have a plan for maximizing my strengths and minimizing my weaknesses.	1	2	3	4	5	6	7	8	9	10

Now, add up all your scores to get a sense of where you are today, and what areas you might want to focus more on going forward. The higher your score in each category, the more closely you are aligned with the story of you. As time goes by, take this assessment again and chart your progress.

The Story Of You

It is time to begin your journey. You have already seen most of these questions in the previous chapters. You may or may not have answered them in those sections. Now is your chance to re-assess each dimension and answer these questions for yourself as you build up the elements of the story of you. Return now to each of the twelve dimensions of the story of you, and document your truths on the following pages.

Purpose

What activities are you most passionate about?

_____

_____

_____

_____

_____

What skills that are you most proud of, which give you the most personal satisfaction?

_____

_____

_____

_____

_____

Which of your skills or activities have had the most positive feedback from others?

_____

_____

_____

On a scale of 1 to 10, rate the activities you enjoy doing against your level of passion for them, your level of skill, and the level of feedback you've received about them.

Activity you enjoy.	Passion Rank	Skill Rank	Feedback Rank	Total

Using a blank sheet of paper, draw a 3D box similar to the one on page 74. Which of your highlighted activities has the highest overall position in that 3D matrix view of passion, skills, and feedback?

_____

If you were given $20 Million dollars and 10 years to live, write down what you would do with the money and the time.

_____

_____

_____

Going forward, the following activities should be part of my life's purpose.

_____

_____

_____

In once sentence, *this* is my life's purpose.

_____

_____

_____

Is your purpose above congruent with what you are doing today?

_____

Personality

How would you describe your behavior and personality? If you've taken psychological assessments in the past, include what you've learned about your personality here:

_____

_____

_____

Write down the three best aspects of your personality.

_____

_____

_____

How would those who know you or work closest with you describe your behavior? Ask three people to tell you three things they think are best about your personality. Write them down.

_____

_____

_____

_____

_____

Ask three people to tell you three things you should change in your interactions with people in life or at work. Write them down.

_____

_____

_____

_____

_____

_____

Think of some defining, catalytic events that have happened in your personal and professional life. How did you respond to them? What do these experiences exemplify about your personality?

_____

_____

_____

_____

_____

Ask three people to recall some experiences they've shared with you that could be used to exemplify certain aspects of your personality. Write them down.

_____

_____

_____

_____

_____

Lessons

Think back to all the different jobs or business ventures you've ever had. In the following table, write each one down, and write down why you started it, why you left it, and what unique lesson(s) you learned from each experience:

Year	Vocation	Why did you start?	Why did it end?	Lesson(s) Learned?

What do you care most about? What aspect of all the lessons you've learned are deal-breakers for you in future decisions? What must you have in any business venture you are involved in?

_____

_____

_____

_____

What have you discovered yourself to be? Are you a good team player? Employee? Entrepreneur? Investor? Are you an innovator or an adapter? Write down what you've learned about your unique work style and preferences:

_____

_____

_____

_____

_____

_____

What have you learned about your life outside of work?

_____

_____

_____

_____

_____

What have you learned about your relationships with people?

_____

_____

_____

_____

_____

Context

Based on reviewing your passion, skills and feedback, the purpose of your life and work is:

Your personality consists of the following strengths and weaknesses, which you will maximize and minimize respectively:

Strengths:

Weaknesses:

_____

_____

The lessons you have learned about yourself through your past life and business decisions are:

_____

_____

_____

_____

_____

Challenges

Write down the current challenges in your life, each followed by the pros, the cons, and the opportunity inherent in each difficulty:

Challenge	Cons	Pros	Conversion

How is your life's purpose affected by these challenges?

_____

_____

_____

_____

_____

How will you maximize the strengths and minimize the weaknesses in your personality as you address these challenges?

_____

_____

_____

_____

_____

_____

What is your level of urgency? How much do you *want* change? Are you inspired and motivated to turn these challenges into advantages in the service of your purpose? Why or why not?

_____

_____

_____

_____

Change

Write down the change you need to implement in your own story in order to get the results you seek:

_____

_____

_____

_____

_____

_____

As you pursue the change you seek, what specific *actions* will you take in order to capitalize on your strengths?

_____

_____

_____

As you pursue the change you seek, what specific things will you do less of in order to minimize your weaknesses?

_____

_____

_____

Change won't happen unless you have a burning, personal business case. *Why* are you willing to do the hard work involved in changing and pursuing my goals?

_____

_____

_____

_____

_____

Using the S.T.O.R.Y. strategy and scorecard process, measure your progress:

Stakeholders:

Are you addressing the stakeholders who really need your service? Are you fulfilling their needs?

_____

_____

Transformation:

Are you leading and influencing your stakeholders based on *their* needs, or yours?

_____

_____

Orchestration:

Have you systematized your work processes so that they can work without you? Are you involving others in your processes?

Resources:

Are you utilizing your full, God-given talents? Are you expressing your creativity?

You:

Are you spending enough time to develop yourself further as a contributor or leader?

Who will you explain your desired changes to, and from whom will you periodically request feedback:

Conclusion

Visualize what your life would be like in the conclusion phase of your story. Write it down:

_____

_____

_____

_____

_____

Pretend that you are one of the two people in our earlier story whose dream was to live on a hill. Are you living on that hill today, or working at another job, (such as driving a taxicab), as a means of making enough money to eventually live on the hill?

_____

_____

_____

_____

_____

Write down three external derailers of which you should be careful.

_____

_____

_____

_____

_____

_____

Write down three derailers within your personality of which you should be aware.

_____

_____

_____

_____

_____

Write down your plan to fortify yourself emotionally using the A.B.C. of emotional power:

Attitude:

What will you do to keep your attitude positive?

_____

_____

_____

Belief:

What will you do to fortify and strengthen your belief in your own self-story and personal mission?

_____

Care:

What will you do to take care of your dreams so that nothing can distract you?

Contribution

Now it is time to write down what your contribution will be. Start with the end in mind. What will be the crux of your story? What will be the moral of your story? Someday, when your story is told, the following will be the moral of that story – the *point* of your story:

When your story is told, the following will have been your contribution to your family.

When your story is told, the following will have been your contribution to the world of work.

Self-Story

Now the time has come to *write* your Self-Story. This is what all of our worksheets and questions so far have been preparing you for. Starting with your purpose, and based on all the information you've collected so far, use the five acts structure to organize and summarize your *Story Of You*:

Context: (purpose, personality, and lessons)

_____

_____

_____

_____

_____

_____

Challenge: (opportunities, and urgency for change)

_____

_____

_____

_____

_____

_____

Change: (what actions you will take in different areas of life)

Conclusion: (starting with the end in mind, what success looks like for you)

Contribution: (what you will given to the world)

_____

_____

_____

_____

_____

_____

_____

Now, read your self-story once a day. Remember that this is a living document, meaning it should evolve as you do. Paste a copy of it strategically in places where your eyes will find it at home and at work. Do this for at least a month. Very soon, every single word in your mission statement will be adopted by your unconscious powers and you'll be on your way to a successful implementation of the story of you.

Goals

Write down one of your primary goals:

_____

_____

Now write down the sub-tasks that will support your primary goal. Arrange them into three categories. Strikers are those sub-tasks that are directly related to your primary goal. Midfielders are those sub-tasks that are designed to help you take advantage of existing or unforeseen challenges and turn them into opportunities and advantages. Defenders are those sub-tasks designed to keep you aware of, and defend you from opponents that are working against you, trying to derail you from outside, as well as inside.

Strikers:

_____

_____

_____

_____

_____

_____

Midfielders:

_____

_____

_____

_____

_____

_____

Defenders:

_____

_____

_____

_____

_____

_____

_____

Weaknesses

What are your weaknesses?

_____

_____

_____

_____

_____

What consequences are these weaknesses producing in your life?

_____

_____

_____

_____

_____

What will you do to minimize these weaknesses?

_____

_____

_____

_____

_____

Whom will you declare your plans to for support and feedback?

_____

_____

_____

_____

_____

Strengths

What are your strengths?

_____

_____

_____

_____

_____

What advantages do your strengths produce in your life?

_____

_____

_____

_____

_____

What will you do to maximize these strengths?

_____

_____

_____

_____

_____

To whom will you declare your plans for support and feedback?

_____

_____

_____

_____

_____

About The Author

Dr. Pelè Raymond Ugboajah is a leadership development author, educator, coach, and songwriter. His leadership development methodology involves a mix of organizational development psychology and the real-life lessons he has learned from his own circuitous story.

Born and raised in a war-torn African refugee village, he was named after Pelè of Brazil – the greatest soccer player on earth – whose influence was so great that it stopped a civil war for two days in 1967. Inspired by the myth of his namesake, Pelè Raymond refused to believe that his own dreams were impossible. With nothing but the clothes on his back and a head full of passion, he overcame numerous obstacles and began a journey from third world poverty to the highest reaches of the American dream.

Pelè is an avid innovator, storyteller and musician, and has worked for over 15 years in various corporate leadership positions and entrepreneurial ventures. Starting out as a corporate 'evangelist', he helped to create a $200 million dollar business by giving software sales presentations to leading companies across the globe. Later, as director of marketing at a $20-billion-dollar company, he led a global effort to establish the corporation as a leader in the enterprise software marketplace.

Pelè holds an MBA and a PhD in the field of leadership development, and maintains an enduring passion for writing and creating music. Over the years, he has authored several books and songs, and has spoken to diverse business audiences. In 1996, Pelè produced six songs for Alexander O'Neal's EMI Billboard #58 album, and in 2006, he became the Toastmasters District 6 Champion of Public Speaking.

Today, through innovative motivation, music, and mentoring programs, Pelè helps leaders find purpose, success, and fulfillment in their lives and work, and spurs them on to live their dreams and achieve their highest potential.

For more information about:

- Getting a complimentary LeaderPractice consultation session.
- Hiring Pelè as a keynote speaker.
- Obtaining Pelè's songs from the 'Story Of You' Soundtrack.

Please visit www.LeaderPractice.com.

References

Academy of Achievement. (2008). *Sir Roger Bannister.* Retrieved December 16, 2008, from http://www.achievement.org/autodoc/page/ban0pro-1

Arntz, W., Chase, B., & Vicente, M. (Producers), & Vicente, M., Chase, B., & Arntz, W. (Directors). (2004). *What the bleep do we know!* [Motion picture]. United States: Lord of the Wind Films.

Braley, B. (1916). *Things as they are: Ballads.* New York: George H. Doran Company.

British Broadcasting Corporation. (2003) *BBC News: Nigeria tops happiness survey.* Retrieved December 16, 2008, from http://news.bbc.co.uk/2/hi/africa/3157570.stm

British Broadcasting Corporation. (2004). Pigeons reveal map-reading secret. Retrieved December, 12, 2008 from http://news.bbc.co.uk/2/hi/uk_news/3460977.stm

Cable News Network. (2008). *Wearing 'almost homeless' sign, ex-executive seeks work.* Retrieved December 11, 2008, from http://www.cnn.com/2008/LIVING/12/05/unemployed.sign/

Campbell, J. (1990). *The hero's journey: Joseph Campbell on his life and work.* New York: New World Library.

CareerBuilder. (2006). *Fifty-Seven Percent of Hiring Managers Say They Have Caught a Lie on a Resume, CareerBuilder.com Survey Finds.* Retrieved December 8, 2008, from http://www.careerbuilder.com/share/aboutus/pressreleasesdetail.aspx?id=pr330&sd=10%2F17%2F2006&ed=12%2F31%2F2006

Carter-Scott, C. (1998). If life is a game, these are the rules: Ten rules for being human as introduced in Chicken Soup for the Soul. New York: Broadway Books.

Colman, A. (2001). *A dictionary of psychology.* United Kingdom: Oxford University Press.

Covey, S. R. (1989). *The 7 habits of highly effective people: powerful lessons in personal change.* New York: Free Press.

Dijksterhuis, A., Nordgren, L. (2006). A theory of unconscious thought. *Association of Psychological Science, 2*(1), 95-109.

ExecuNet. (2007). *15ᵗʰ Annual Executive Job Market Intelligence Report.* Retrieved December 10, 2008, from http://www.execunet.com/promo/pdf/EUN2007Survey_su mmary.pdf.

Haidt, J. (2006). *The happiness hypothesis: Finding modern truth in ancient wisdom.* New York: Basic Books.

HR Policy Association. (2008). *2008 Annual Chief Human Resource Officer Survey.* Paper presented at the annual meeting of the HR Policy Association, Boca Raton, FL.

Jennings, C. (2007). *70:20:10 Rule: Conspiracy of convenience.* Paper presented at the Global Summit 2006, Australia. Retrieved from http://www.microassist.com/ELearning/ELearningResource s/tabid/142/EntryID/39/Default.aspx

Lee, M. (1998). The Goethe Society of North America: Quotes-Commitment. Retrieved December 13, 2008 from http://www.goethesociety.org/pages/quotescom.html

Maltz, M. (1960). *Psycho-cybernetics: A new way to get more living out of life.* New York: Pocket Books.

Matthews, G. (2008). Goals research summary. Retrieved Dember 16, 2008 from http://www.dominican.edu/academics/facultypages/gailmatt hews/researchsummary2.pdf

MSNBC. (2008). *Alabama van driver headed to Nobel ceremony.* Retrieved December 15, 2008 from http://www.msnbc.msn.com/id/28056265/

PR Newswire. (2008). *Problems at the top: Apathy, contempt for managers.* Retrieved December 13, 2008, from http://www.prnewswire.com/cgi-bin/stories.pl?ACCT=109&STORY=/www/story/01-21-2005/0002869774&EDATE=

Stanford News Service. (2005). Text of Steve Jobs' commencement address, 2005. Retrieved December 16, 2008 from http://news-service.stanford.edu/news/2005/june15/jobs-061505.html

The New Yorker. (2008). *Why Me? Alec Baldwin's dissapointment, undimmed by success.* Retrieved December 10, 2008 from http://www.newyorker.com/reporting/2008/09/08/080908f a_fact_parker?currentPage=all

Time. (1999). *Time 100: Pele.* Retrieved December 15, 2008 from http://www.time.com/time/time100/heroes/profile/pele01. html